EVALUATING HUMAN RELATIONS PROGRAMS FOR

INDUSTRIAL FOREMEN AND SUPERVISORS

EVALUATING HUMAN RELATIONS PROGRAMS FOR
INDUSTRIAL FOREMEN AND SUPERVISORS

By

DONALD LEE KIRKPATRICK

A Thesis Submitted in Partial Fulfillment
of the Requirements for the Degree of
DOCTOR OF PHILOSOPHY
At the
UNIVERSITY OF WISCONSIN

1954

ISBN 978-145285-033-7

A Note to the Reader

This is a reprinting of the original dissertation of Donald
L. Kirkpatrick exactly as it was written in 1954. No changes or
updates have been made to the original manuscript.
This is considered the beginnings of the Kirkpatrick Model as it
is known today.
Kirkpatrick Partners hopes you find this document
practical, interesting, and enjoyable to read.

ACKNOWLEDGEMENTS

My deepest appreciation goes to my wife, Fern Kirkpatrick, whose patience, encouragement, and assistance made this study possible.

I should like to extend my sincere thanks to Dr. A. H. Edgerton, major professor, whose constant guidance and constructive criticism were extremely helpful.

Dr. D. W. Belcher also deserves my appreciation because of his able assistance in the selection and development of the investigation.

Others who were always willing to help include Dr. A.S. Barr, Dr. C. W. Harris, Dr. J. W. M. Rothney, and Professor Philip Fox. To them I should like to express my sincere thanks for suggestions on various aspects of the study.

I am also indebted to Dr. R. L. Moberly, Dr. M. Gordon, and Dr. E. E. Jennings whose advice and help contributed much to the investigation.

Finally, I should like to thank the staff of the Industrial Management Institute of the University of Wisconsin, those from the two private companies who cooperated, and the students in the seminars who constructively criticized the progress of the study.

TABLE OF CONTENTS

CHAPTER

LIST OF TABLES

CHAPTER I

NATURE AND SCOPE OF THE STUDY

Statement of the Problem

Human relations programs for foremen and supervisors are considered the most popular type of training conducted by various industries throughout the United States, according to a recent survey of members of the American Society of Training Directors (53). Foremen and supervisors have been selected as the persons most in need of this training because of the key position they occupy between management and the workers. Most companies have concluded that the principal job of their foremen is to maintain high production through the proper handling of the workers. These programs, therefore, have been designed to provide the supervisor with a better understanding of the employees--their interests, personalities, capacities, drives--and to motivate the supervisor to apply this understanding in order to maintain high morale and peak production.

A survey of the research conducted in human relations training reveals that there have been a limited number of objective attempts to determine the effectiveness of these programs. Training directors are generally agreed that there is urgent need for such evaluation. However, they have neglected the evaluation either because of their lack of knowledge of techniques or because they feel they are too busy conducting the programs to find the necessary time to determine the actual results.

An example of the type of program that is being conducted throughout the United States is the Institute on Human Relations for Foremen and Supervisors which is presented approximately fifteen times a year by the Industrial Management Institute of the University of Wisconsin. Large-scale participation by representatives from companies located in Wisconsin and nearby states seems to indicate that the attending foremen and supervisors derive considerable satisfaction and some benefit from attending these Institutes. Comment sheets filled out by the enrollees clearly reveal an enthusiastic approval of the program. However, until the present study was undertaken, there had been no objective attempt to measure what specific facts and principles are being learned by the participants.

Since the Institute is designed to provide facts, ideas, and principles which will enable the supervisors to do a better job of handling their employees, there is an obvious need for determining how much of this particular information is understood and accepted. Consequently, this investigation is an attempt to evaluate the changes in knowledge that result from attendance at these University Institutes. In addition, the Human Relations Training Programs of two private companies were studied in order to determine their relative effectiveness.

Background of the Problem

The University of Wisconsin is one of the few universities which regularly offer human relations programs for industrial foremen and supervisors. To this writer's knowledge, Marquette University and Southern Methodist University are the only other higher educational institutions now offering similar programs.

Private industries from coast to coast, however, are concentrating more on human relations programs than any other type of training (53). An examination of the programs of such companies as A. O. Smith Corporation, International Harvester Company, Abbot Laboratories, Wisconsin Electric Power Company, and the United States Rubber Company reveals that the subject content and the techniques of the University Institutes are similar to those used in private companies.

Since research on evaluation of human relations programs is very limited, it is hoped that the techniques and findings of this study will prove useful not only to the organizations involved but also to companies who continue to offer basic programs for the improvement of the total performance of their foremen and supervisors.

History of the University Institutes

The Industrial Management Institute of the University of Wisconsin has been charged with the responsibility of conducting Human Relations Institutes for industrial foremen and supervisors since the fall of 1944. These programs were first inaugurated because the Engineering Science Management War Training Program of the United States Government requested this University, along with several others, to provide a short intensive course in human relations for new foremen. The demand was so great

4

that this special Institute was repeated twenty-two times during the first year.

After one year, the federal government no longer continued to sponsor such programs. A number of companies which believed that their foremen had received definite benefits from participation in the first-year program requested the University to continue the Institutes on a fee basis. Beginning in 1945, companies were required to pay thirty-five dollars for each foreman or supervisor who was enrolled in the program. Every year thereafter, from ten to fifteen Institutes on Human Relations for Foremen and Supervisors were offered in order to meet the demand of industries and businesses from Wisconsin and nearby states.

During the first ten years in which these Institutes were offered, little change took place in subject matter, techniques, or scheduled. The length of the program was four and one-half days or approximately thirty hours. The subject matter invariably included: duties and responsibilities of a supervisor; understanding people; employee attitudes; solving a human relations problem; the supervisor as an instructor; and leadership.

About half of these sessions were conducted by business and industrial leaders who were selected on the basis of education, experience, and ability to conduct an informal conference. The remainder of the sessions was led by regularly appointed staff members of the Industrial Management Institute. The guided discussion technique rather than the scheduled lecture was made the primary foundation of the program. This technique was adopted because it was felt that foremen and supervisors were more apt to accept the ideas and suggestions of other foremen and supervisors than those of the instructors alone. Then too, it was assumed that the interest and motivation of the enrollees would be higher if they participated in the discussion instead of listening to lectures hour after hour. Also, this method served as an assurance that the program would be practical, because those in attendance were eager and qualified to talk about their plant experiences and problems. The lecture method was employed only when new material was presented to the group. Frequent use was made of such instructional aids as films, the blackboard, and case studies.

Groups were limited in size to twenty-five participants in order to allow for maximum discussion by enrollees. Representatives from companies of many sizes and types were enrolled in each Institute. The majority of the persons attending were first level foremen and supervisors, but attendance by staff management, superintendents, and plant managers was not uncommon.

Between two and three thousand persons attended these Institutes from 1945 to 1953 at a cost to business and industry of approximately seven hundred and fifty thousand dollars. In order to obtain an indication of enrollee reaction, the staff prepared comment sheets which were completed by each participant at the end of the Institute sessions. These sheets were constantly revised by Institute staff members in order to get more objective comments on subject matter and the performance of the discussion leaders. The annual field calls on participating companies provided additional opportunity for determining the reaction to the programs. The personnel managers and executives who were contacted on these calls seemed to feel that the program was worthwhile, but no one reported an attempt to determine just how much the supervisors had learned or whether or not their on-the-job performance had shown specific improvement.

There seems to be no doubt that the enrollees enjoyed the Institute sessions. Their comments consistently revealed how much they liked the program, but there was little indication of the actual benefits they had received.

Currently there is an increasing cost consciousness on the part of business and industry. Training is being looked upon rather skeptically with such comments as: "Are you sure it pays off?" If the University of Wisconsin's Human Relations Institutes are going to continue to attract industrial foremen and supervisors, there is an urgent need to determine by objective means the particular benefits that are derived. There also must be a means of ascertaining the knowledges and the attitudes that the enrollees bring to the program. It must be determined whether or not the attitudes toward their jobs are being changed by participation in the Institutes. Only with this kind and quality of information can these programs be analyzed satisfactorily in terms of their existing weaknesses and subsequent improvement.

Definition of Terms

In this study, the following frequently used terms will convey the specific meanings as described:

1. "Human Relations" Programs and Institutes will be used to include such general topics or subject areas as: duties and responsibilities of supervisors; understanding people; supervisor and

employee attitudes; how to solve a problem; how to train employees; and the supervisor as a leader. Each of these programs is designed to improve the performance of industrial supervisors by providing them with facts, principles, and techniques related to the human aspects of their jobs.

2. "Foremen" and "Supervisor" will be used interchangeably to refer to the lowest level of industrial management. He is directly responsible for supervising the rank and file production workers. In some companies he is called a foreman while in others he is known as a supervisor.

3. "Test" and "Inventory" will be used interchangeably to refer to the one hundred item SUPERVISORY INVENTORY ON HUMAN RELATIONS which was constructed by the investigator.

4. "Pretest" will refer to the Inventory which each foreman completed at the beginning of the program he attended.

5. "Posttest" will refer to the Inventory which each foreman completed immediately following the program.

The Scope of the Study

The primary purpose of this study at the outset was to evaluate several similar human relations training programs for industrial foremen and supervisors. During the course of the investigation, however, it seemed advisable to seek the answer to several related questions as well. Therefore, five different but related problems were included in the scope of this investigation. Chief emphasis was placed on the first of these five problems which are listed below:

1. How Effective are Human Relations Programs in Imparting Knowledge and Changing Attitudes of Industrial Foremen and Supervisors?

   The SUPERVISORY INVENTORY ON HUMAN RELATIONS was administered to the foremen before and after each program being studied. A comparison of pretest and posttest responses indicates the effectiveness of the program.

2. How Valid is the SUPERVISORY INVENTORY ON HUMAN RELATIONS As a Measure of Job Performance?

   The foremen and supervisors of two private companies were ranked on the basis of their on-the-job performance. These ranks were related to Inventory pretest scores to determine the ability of the test to measure job performance.

3. Which Items on the Inventory Can Be Used in the Selection of Supervisors?

   The responses to each of the one hundred items on the inventory were compared with the rankings of the supervisors in the two companies to determine which ones discriminate between "good" and "poor" foremen. An inventory consisting of these items can then be used as a valid device for selecting new supervisors.

4. Which Foremen Seem to Benefit Most from Human Relations Training?

   The gains in Inventory scores from pretest to posttest were correlated with personal characteristics of the foremen. These characteristics included age, education, years of company experience, years of supervisory experience, number of employees supervised, and performance on the job.

5. <u>What Subject Matter Should Be Emphasized in Future University Institutes?</u>

A tabulation of the incorrect responses to the pretest reveals the knowledges and attitudes that foremen and supervisors bring to the University Institutes. An analysis of these responses indicates the subject matter that should be stressed by Institute instructors in future programs.

These five questions, then, provide the problems which were considered in this investigation. A detailed description of the programs, the measuring instrument, and the techniques used will be included in Chapter III. Before discussing these materials and methods, however, it seems necessary to examine the pertinent literature in the following chapter. A study of this research, concerned with the evaluation of human relations training programs, will reveal why certain procedures and methods were adopted for this investigation.

CHAPTER II

REVIEW OF PERTINENT RESEARCH

Evaluation of human relations training programs has been
generally neglected by directors of these programs. It
also is notable that such well known writers as Aspley and
Whitmore (2), Knowles and Thompson (27), Moore (39), and
Pigors and Meyers (44) discuss the subject of supervisory
training but fail to include any mention of the need for
evaluating results of such programs.

It is encouraging to find that evidence on the validity of
these programs is stressed by other writers. Planty (45),
a practitioner as well as a writer in the field of
training, states: "Some system of evaluation must be
instituted if supervisory training is to justify its
existence." Tiffin (52) makes the following observation:
"Without.... measurement, there is no way of knowing
whether the training is worth what it costs, or indeed,
whether it is worth anything at all."

A variety of methods and techniques for evaluating human
relations programs has been recommended. Jucius (21)
suggests a number of approaches to the problem. He
recommends that objective measurements are desirable, but
he points out that it is most difficult to attribute
objective results to training alone. Jurgensen (22) also
recognizes the difficulties involved in using objective
techniques. Planty, Efferson, and McCord (46) emphasize

that completely objective evaluation of training is frequently difficult and must often be based on "the keen business judgment of experienced leaders." Beckman (3) believes that objective evidences are the most valuable in determining the effectiveness of human relations programs but reports that attitude and opinion measures are most frequently used. He feels that "the opinion of those in training can be determined at the close of a training course and used as an index of evaluation."

The best way to show training results is to prove that improved performance takes place, according to Keachie (26). He recommends the use of a control group and an experimental group, matched on the basis of such characteristics as age, sex, and education. Keachie mentions that a pretest and posttest of the group being trained have usually been used instead of the control and experimental groups because of the difficulty of securing such ideal controls in an industrial situation.

Solomon (49) goes so far as to advocate the use of two control groups in certain kinds of experimental studies. This method is believed by him to be particularly applicable to the evaluation of human relations training. In the case of a pretest and posttest evaluation, he recommends the following procedure:

	Experimental Group	Control Group 1	Control Group 2
Pretest	Yes	Yes	No
Training	Yes	No	Yes
Posttest	Yes	Yes	Yes

His essential reasoning is that in the case of Control Group 1, there are effects of the pretest which influence the scores on the posttest even though no training is received. These effects may be either positive or negative in nature, Solomon believes.

In an article called "The Research Approach to Training," McGehee (35) recommends that programs be developed and evaluated by means of objective techniques. Production criteria should be used to determine the effectiveness whenever possible, he states. To evaluate instruction techniques, McGehee suggests that matched groups be taught the same subject matter by different techniques.

Specific attempts to evaluate human relations training programs will be divided into subjective and objective types for analysis purposes. The former category will include appraisals by instructors of the programs as well as studies in which verbal or written comments were elicited from those who received the training. Objective evaluation will consist of investigations in which evidence of improvement was sought by measuring attitudes, knowledges, production records, or other criteria.

Subjective Evaluation

Habbe (15) reports on a program conducted at the Bigelow-Sanford Carpet Company. He states: ".... but a combination of good features seems to be producing excellent results. At least the company is well satisfied and the meetings are bringing the foremen and management closer together and this result, in itself, more than justifies the program."

Maier (33) conducted a program in which psychological principles were stressed in order to influence supervisory attitudes. He states: "It is believed that the program has proved itself successful in its objectives and it is now being extended to management employees at all levels of supervision.... The supervisors themselves found their jobs are more interesting after training than before. They felt they had better control of the situation; they enjoyed the work more and they found themselves to be less on the defensive."

A common technique used by industries to measure the results of human relations programs is the posttraining questionnaire which is submitted to recipients of the training. The questions are usually quite general and attempt to get supervisory reactions to such questions as:

Did you feel the program was worthwhile?
What subjects did you enjoy the most?
How would you rate the conference leader?
What did you get out of the program?

These should probably be classified as comment sheets rather than an evaluation device. However, this is the extent of many attempts to evaluate training programs in the area of human relations.

In an unpublished study conducted at the Marathon Corporation of Neenah, Wisconsin, King Evans, Training Manager, surveyed one hundred ninety supervisors from six plants in order to determine the effectiveness of the human relations training course he had conducted. His questionnaire was designed to obtain supervisory reaction to: subjects and materials; presentation and discussion;

the conference leader; and the overall program. The final items on the questionnaire concerned the application of the training program to their jobs as supervisors. An analysis of the responses showed that the program was well received by those in attendance. Ninety-seven per cent of the supervisors indicated that they had tried to put at least one principle into practice. Seventy per cent said they had tried to put most of them into practice with a fair amount of success. One of the specific purposes of the Marathon program was to improve a personal habit of each supervisor. At the conclusion of the program, ninety-four per cent replied that they were trying to improve one of their poor habits.

A training program conducted for municipal supervisors in the city of Columbia, Missouri, was appraised by Taylor (51) in 1951. One of the techniques he used was the administration of questionnaires to the participants at the conclusion of the program. Anonymous responses revealed: "the supervisors enjoyed the sessions; they liked the films and aids that were used; they appreciated the opportunity to get to know their fellow supervisors better; and they felt that the one-hour sessions were desirable." An additional indication of the value of the program came from the fact that the supervisors got together before and after the meetings for "off-stage" arguments. Randomly selected interviews with the supervisors also revealed that the conferences were beneficial.

Osterberg and Lindbom (42) used the "ask him" approach in their study conducted in 1952. They mailed an evaluative questionnaire to each supervisor who had participated in the human relations training program in an oil company. The answers of ninety per cent of the supervisors that responded stated that they were doing things differently on the job because of the program. Replies to another question indicated that sixty-five per cent of the supervisors who returned the questionnaires had observed changes in the performance of the workers under them. Osterberg and Lindbom conclude that some evaluation is better than none. They suggest that an evaluation design should be built into the training program. They also recognize the limitation that "the industrial situation simply does not lend itself well to controlled experiments."

These subjective attempts to evaluate human relations training are preferable to no evaluation. However, because of the limitations of subjective techniques, they should be used only when objective evaluation is not practical.

Objective Evaluation

Within the past few years there has been an increasing effort on the part of investigators to use objective techniques in evaluating human relations programs. The most frequently used measuring instrument has been HOW SUPERVISE? which is a paper-and-pencil inventory developed by File and Remmers (9). It was used at the Industrial Tape Corporation by Weiland (54) and revealed an average improvement in test scores of eighteen per cent resulting from attendance at the supervisory training course. Katzell (24) conducted a course dealing with human relations principles and applications. He found a significant gain in scores on HOW SUPERVISE?

File and Remmers (10) report in the manual for use with their test a study of five hundred eighty-nine supervisors in the rubber industry. Significant increases were found on the posttest. Mahler (32) reports another study in which HOW SUPERVISE? was used to measure the effectiveness of the program. This study showed that the supervisory training course on "Human Relations" at an RCA Victor plant produced positive changes in mean scores from pretest to posttest.

Several investigators have attempted to test the validity of HOW SUPERVISE?. Weitz and Nuckols (55) found that scores on the test were not valid in predicting turnover or production in a life insurance company. File (8) found that scores on the test show a +.35 correlation with education. Millard (38) discovered that the test correlate +.71 with the intelligence of factory foremen. In another study, Maloney (34) analyzed its reading difficulty by using the Flesch formula. He concluded that the mean reading difficulty is of high-school-graduate level, and that the test is of doubtful value for foremen with less education. Wickert (57) reached the same conclusion concerning its validity for foremen with less than a high school education.

Mahler (32) reports that in a large mid-western insurance company, four different techniques were used in order to evaluate a supervisory training program. First of all, the superiors rated the performance of the supervisors before and after the training and indicated very little change. Secondly, a self-evaluation rating by a group of thirty supervisors showed that fifty-two per cent felt they had improved their performance. The third technique, a study of the turnover rate of employees showed considerable reduction from pretraining to posttraining, but so many factors could have influenced the situation that it is problematical if it could have been attributed to the training alone. A fourth and final effort was made to measure the results by the administration of HOW SUPERVISE? before and after the training. The results of this testing procedure revealed that a greater percentage of supervisors obtained a lower score following the course than showed equal or greater scores. The difference was significant.

In a study at the International Harvester Company in 1950, Fleishman (11) found that the Supervisory Behavior Description, administered to supervisors before and after the human relations training, revealed significant positive changes. After the training, the foremen scored higher on "consideration" which was defined as the extent to which the leader is considerate of those under him. However, in the plant situation, he found a significant decrease in the application of the consideration attitude to the workers. Fleishman concluded that this discrepancy suggests that a foreman may learn different attitudes for each situation. He also states that the kind of boss under whom the foreman worked seemed highly related to the attitudes and behavior of the foremen.

In a study of a supervisory program on human relations at the Farm Bureau Insurance Company of Columbus, Ohio, Canter (4) administrated a selected battery of six tests before and after the training to an experimental group and a control group. The experimental group received the training while the control group did not. From a comparison of pretest and posttest scores and from the intercorrelations between test scores and performance rankings, Canter concludes:

1. Facts and principles concerning psychological aspects of behavior and group functioning were learned by the supervisors receiving the training.

2. Following the training, supervisors tended to be more "sensitized to behavioral acts, expressions of attitudes, and group differences" of their employees.

An extensive and well-planned study was reported by Jennings (20) in 1954 on the results of a supervisory training program conducted at the Monsanto Chemical Company of St. Louis, Missouri. The objectives of the program were based on the three most desirable qualities of supervisors that had been determined by Jennings in a previous study (19). These qualities included:

1. Give clear-cut instructions.
2. Be fair to the workers.
3. Go to bat for the workers.

The Jennings Supervisory Analysis was administered to employees before the program began. It was completed by the same employees one year after the first administration and six months after completion of the training program. He found that the before-and-after evaluation of successful foremen correlated +.60 whereas similar correlation for unsuccessful foremen was +.31. Further analysis of the evaluation of the changes in the unsuccessful foremen revealed that "giving clear-cut instructions" and "being fair to the workers" showed considerable improvement while "going to bat for the workers" showed no change. Jennings concluded that the unsuccessful foremen, those most in need of change, showed improvement in two of the three qualities considered most desirable by their employees.

Mahler (32) reported one of the most extensive investigations that has been made to evaluate a human relations training program. It was carried out by the Survey Research Center of the University of Michigan. The purpose of the experiment was to measure the effects of a program conducted at the Detroit Edison Company. Measurement of employee satisfaction as well as supervisory self-appraisal were used to evaluate the training.

The training program was continued from September, 1949, through June, 1950, and included three phases:

1. Dr. Norman Maier, Professor of Psychology at the University of Michigan, presented a series of twelve three-hour lectures at three week intervals. He made the sessions lively and interesting by interspersing skits, movies, role playing, and group participation.

2. Maier conducted a series of meetings with selected management personnel who were to assist in the application of the lecture material to the job. These persons also had attended the lectures and were superiors of the supervisors being studied. The purpose of these meetings was to prepare these superiors to lead on-the-job discussions on the application of the principles expounded in Maier's lectures.

3. The final phase of the Human Relations Training Program was an on-the-job discussion of how the human relations principles could be used.

20

Self-appraisal of an experimental and a control group of supervisors was made before and after the training. In addition, the employees who were supervised by the two groups completed an attitude questionnaire before and after the program. An analysis of results of both measures showed little evidence of improvement in on-the-job-performance.

The following conclusions were reported in connection with this study:

1. Employee attitudes will be most improved when the foreman is motivated to change and when the "climate" within which he operates is conducive to change.

2. Human relations programs are most effective when the attitudes and practices of higher management are consistent with course content.

3. Attitudinal and behavioral changes in foremen can better be measured by perceptions of subordinates than by changes in responses of foremen themselves.

In 1952, Lindbom (30) attempted to evaluate the effects of a supervisory training program in human relations through before-and-after measurement of employee attitudes. The study was carried out in the home office of a small insurance company in the Mid West. The group being studied consisted of twenty-five first-line supervisors.

Alternate forms of HOW SUPERVISE? were administered as part of the first and final training meetings in order to measure the change in knowledge and attitudes. In addition, the attitudes of employees under their supervision were measured by means of a questionnaire administered prior to the beginning of and three months after the conclusion of the program. The reason for the three-month delay was "to lessen the possible effect of a temporarily high supervisor enthusiasm during the period of the course which might diminish with time."

The attitude questionnaire that was administered to the employees was developed at the Industrial Relations Center of the University of Minnesota. It consisted of thirteen incomplete statements which required the employee to check one of five categories ranging from "Excellent" to "Very Poor," and one hundred forty-four complete statements followed by five choices ranging from "Strongly Agree" to Strongly Disagree." Eight sub-scales as well as a total score scale were obtained. These sub-scales measure specific attitudes toward the company, communications, co-workers, hours and pay, supervisor, type of work, working conditions, and the overall job.

The supervisors showed a significant increase in mean score from pretest to posttest of HOW SUPERVISE? Attitudes of employees also were found to be significantly more favorable after the program on all of the scales except hours and pay and working conditions. In analyzing the attitude changes, Lindbom found that women showed more favorable change than men, and new employees showed more favorable change than older, more experienced employees.

Summary of Research

There seems to be a clear indication of the growing interest and effort in the area of evaluation of supervisory training programs on human relations. In 1949, a questionnaire survey (1) was made of members of the American Society of Training Directors to determine which problems in research were most important. Replies were received from two hundred and eighty-three persons representing industry, business, universities, and government. A tabulation of the responses revealed that "the supervisory group in industry is clearly the most important group for which research is needed." Over half of the respondents indicated an interest in the evaluation of supervisory training programs in human relations.

There seems to be a trend for writers in personnel and industrial management to emphasize the need for evaluation. Authors generally agree that techniques should be as objective as possible, but they likewise recognize the barriers to setting up a well-controlled investigation in the industrial situation. They point out that any type of evaluation is probably better than none at all.

The most common form of evaluation used by training personnel is the questionnaire which is completed by the trainees at the conclusion of the program. Where objective methods are used, the test HOW SUPERVISE? has been employed most frequently.

Outstanding investigations have been conducted by Jennings, Lindbom, Fleishman, Canter, and the Survey Research Center of the University of Michigan. Where Jennings, Lindbom, and Canter found generally satisfactory results, Fleishman and the Survey Research Center discovered little evidence that human relations training improved the on-the-job performance of the trainees.

Katzell (25), one of the outstanding writers and practitioners in the evaluation of training programs ably sums up the evidence at hand. He proposes that for best results, the following pattern should be followed: Define the objectives or goals; develop some criterion or yardstick; and compare before and after measures to determine results. More specifically, he recommends the use of paper-and-pencil tests in areas such as human relations where definite sets of performance figures are difficult to obtain. He further states:

> "Such programs typically have among their objectives the increase in certain knowledge or understandings or the modification of certain beliefs or attitudes. A type of yardstick for such programs may, therefore, take the form of a test of the appropriate understandings and attitudes. If the trainees show a gain in knowledge or modification of attitudes in desired directions, then the program may be judged to have been effective."

From this summary and analysis of pertinent research, it is evident that wherever possible, objective methods should be used to evaluate the results of training. In the specific case of human relations programs, it seems best to employ a paper-and-pencil inventory in order to determine the changes that have taken place in the understandings and attitudes of the trainees.

In compliance with the recommendations of the research workers and other writers discussed in this chapter, it was decided to use such a measure to help determine the effectiveness of the programs involved in this study. A detailed description of the measuring instrument and its use will be included in the following chapter.

CHAPTER III

MATERIALS AND METHODS USED IN THIS STUDY

The present Chapter will describe in detail the methods and techniques that were adopted to investigate the five problem questions considered in this study. First, however, it will present descriptions of both the training programs involved and the procedures used in constructing a measuring instrument.

Description of the Programs Being Investigated

University Institutes. These intensive four and one-half day programs were designed and conducted in Madison, Wisconsin, by the staff of the Industrial Management Institute of the University of Wisconsin. They were repeated approximately twelve times each year since 1944 in order to meet the demand of industry from Wisconsin and nearby states. Each Institute started on Monday at 1:00 P.M. and concluded on Friday at 3:30 P.M. A two and one-half hour session and an informal dinner meeting were held on the first day. Approximately six hours of these training meetings were held on each of the other four days.

Objectives. These Institutes were designed to provide facts, principles, and techniques which would be helpful in improving relationships between the foremen and their subordinates.

Subject Content.   The subjects discussed and the amount of time devoted to each are as follows:

The Supervisor's Role in Management	2 hrs.
Understanding People	6 hrs.
The Supervisor and Employee Attitudes	3 hrs.
Solving a Human Relations Problem	3 hrs.
The Supervisor as a Trainer	6 hrs.
The Supervisor as a Leader	3 hrs.
Summary and Discussion of Problems	3 hrs.

(See Exhibit A for a detailed outline of the program.)

It should be noted that the trainees usually got together in the evening in small groups. Human relations problems and experiences were often discussed in these informal "bull sessions."

Techniques.   The basic technique adopted by the staff of the University Institutes might best be called the "guided discussion" technique.   The function of the instructor or discussion leader was to provide background material, present ideas, and then to elicit pertinent comments, suggestions, and experiences from members of the group. The instructor sometimes lectured but the majority of the time was spent in discussion.   The groups were limited in size to twenty-five persons to allow for participation in the discussion by everyone who desired.

In order to supplement this guided discussion, other techniques were employed.   These included:

1. "Buzz" Groups.
   The trainees were divided into groups of about six persons.   After each group had selected a "chairman"

to control the discussion and a "secretary" to record the comments, it proceded to discuss the problem given it by the instructor.

2. Role Playing.

A problem situation involving a supervisor and an employee was discussed, and then role players, selected from the group, would act out the solution.

3. Other Group Participation Techniques.

Some instructors chose additional methods in order to get the trainees to participate in the discussion. One of the most common techniques was to distribute forms for each person to complete. An example of this method was the use of a form entitled, "What Do Workers Want Most From Their Jobs?" (Exhibit B) The supervisors were asked to indicate the order in which they thought workers considered ten job factors to be most important. The results of an actual survey were then given to the group and a discussion followed.

Audio-Visual Aids. The blackboard was used by nearly every discussion leader to write down important points and to record the contributions made by the trainees. In addition, some of the leaders wrote with a black crayon on white flip charts instead of using the blackboard or as a supplement to it. These charts had one advantage over the blackboard in that a completed chart could be removed from sight and referred to later in the session. A few of the instructors introduced a flannel board to make their presentations more effective.

With the exception of the blackboard, the most frequently used aid was the sound motion picture film. (See Exhibit C for a list of films used.)

A recorded case study called "The Case of Harrassed Harry" was played on Wednesday afternoon of each Institute. This was followed by a problem solving discussion. The discussion was usually concluded with one or two role playing situations.

The Discussion Leaders. In each of the Institutes, six different discussion leaders conducted sessions. Usually, four of them were selected from business or industrial firms while the other two were staff men. From a time standpoint, about half of the program was conducted by a member of the staff of the Industrial Management Institute while the other half was led by outside discussion leaders.

Industrial or business men were selected to handle sessions because of past experience at handling similar meetings or because it was felt they could do a satisfactory job. Although no criteria had ever been established upon which to base the selection, the staff man usually considered the person's experience, education, knowledge of supervisory problems, status in the organization, ability to express himself, enthusiasm, and ability to lead a discussion.

The discussion leaders, once confirmed, were sent materials and suggestions on approaches for the handling of the session. Specific techniques and aids that had been used successfully by previous leaders were indicated. The discussion leaders were encouraged to incorporate their own ideas and "gimmicks" into the suggested outline, but they were well oriented to the fact that the "guided discussion" and not the "lecture" method should be the basic technique employed.

The staff men who acted as discussion leaders had been associated with the Institute program for a minimum of two years. During this time they were responsible for: contacting and orienting new discussion leaders; supervising at least three previous Human Relations Institutes and handling numerous sessions in previous Institutes.

Company Programs. Human Relations Training Programs similar to the University Institutes were conducted in two private companies from January, 1953 to June, 1953. One was held in a Wisconsin company and the other in an Iowa corporation.

The Wisconsin paper mill is a two plant operation located in two small cities in the central part of Wisconsin. It employs approximately seventeen hundred persons, most of whom live in one or the other of the small cities. This mill provides the only large scale employment in these communities. The company consists of a pulp mill and a paper mill, and its products include mimeograph and writing papers.

The Iowa manufacturing company is the third largest plant in an industrial city of Iowa with a population of seventy thousand. It employs approximately nine hundred persons and manufactures a number of products including washing machine wringers, aluminum awnings, and refrigerator shelves. Its turnover rate is 2.3 per cent per month.

The programs presented in these companies were similar in nature. They were both conducted by an outside consultant, a different man for the two companies. These two men worked closely together in planning the program, and the one, Dr. Milton Gordon, had learned many of the human relations principles and conference techniques from the other, Dr. Russell Moberly. Therefore, the objectives, subject content, techniques and aids used by both companies can be described together.

Objectives. These programs were designed to provide facts and principles, the acceptance and application of which would improve the relationships between the supervisors and the workers.

Subject Content. The training programs consisted of seven sessions of one and one-half hours each. The subjects covered include the following:

1. The Duties and Responsibilities of a Supervisor
2. The Principles of Organization
3. Understanding Human Behavior
4. Training and Developing Employees
5. Employee-Supervisor Relations
6. Solving a Human Relations Problem
7. Leadership
(See Exhibit D for a more detailed outline.)

The one and one-half hour sessions were conducted one day a week for seven weeks. The groups ranged in size from fifteen to twenty persons. Within each group all of the trainees were of approximately equal level in the organization.

Techniques and Aids. The principal technique used by the instructor was the guided discussion method. The leader presented materials and ideas but much of the time was spent in a discussion of the subject matter. The blackboard was used regularly to record contributions of the group and to write down the main ideas the leader expressed.

Role playing and "buzz" groups were interspersed in the discussion. A recorded case study provided the material for discussion at one of the sessions. Several films were shown during the program.

University Conferences. In January and February of 1954, the Industrial Management Institute of the University of Wisconsin presented a series of four one-day conferences on Human Relations for Foremen and Supervisors in Milwaukee. A similar series of conferences was presented in Racine. These programs were patterned after the University Institutes in regard to objectives, subject content, techniques, aids, and discussion leaders. The main variation from the Institutes was the fact that these conferences were conducted on a one-day a week basis for four weeks rather than for four and one-half consecutive days.

They were presented in these two communities to meet the demand of companies which felt they could spare their foremen for a day at a time but could not afford to let them go to Madison to attend a four and one-half day Institute.

Description of the Supervisors Being Studied

University Institutes.   For this investigation, the six Institutes presented from January to June, 1953, were selected.   They were chosen at the convenience of the investigator and not by any random sampling technique. They were considered to be typical of University Institutes inasmuch as the subject content, techniques, aids, and discussion leaders were basically the same as in all other Institutes.   No attempt was made to determine whether or not the foremen and supervisors in attendance were representative of those who have attended other Institutes. There seems to be little reason to believe that they were not typical, however, because over eighty per cent of them represent companies which continue to participate year after year.   Also, the manner in which the Institutes are announced and publicized has remained basically the same.

Included in the enrollees of the six Institutes selected for this investigation were plant managers, personnel directors, accountants, superintendents, and engineers.   Of the total of one hundred and thirty-five persons who attended, eight-four or sixty-two per cent were classified as foremen or supervisors.   Only these eighty-four subjects were studied in this investigation.   These foremen and supervisors came from twenty-four different companies. Those firms sending the most supervisors to the six Institutes are listed in Exhibit E.

All of the participating firms were manufacturing companies.   They varied in size from less than three hundred to more than four thousand employees.   Their products included beer, tires, outboard motors, motor controls, machine tools, and meat products.

These foremen were found to have an average age of 40.2 years and an education of 11.1 grades. Their company experience averaged 13.1 years while their supervisory experience was found to be 7.8 years. Of the eighty-four foremen, thirty-four had attended previous human relations courses. Some of these programs were in-plant training meetings, while others were conducted by outside-the-plant organizations.

Company Programs. All of the supervisors in both plants were included in this study. In the Wisconsin paper mill there were thirty-four supervisors, while the Iowa manufacturing company consisted of thirty foremen. Sixty per cent of the foremen from the Wisconsin company had attended human relations courses, all of them at the University of Wisconsin Institutes. In the Iowa firm, forty-three per cent had received previous human relations training of one form or another. Additional characteristics of these groups are described in Table I.

TABLE I

AVERAGE CHARACTERISTICS OF SUPERVISORS IN TWO
INDUSTRIAL PLANTS*

	Wisconsin Paper Mill	Iowa Manufacturing Co.
Age	51.6 years	42.2 years
Education	9.8 grades	10.5 grades
Company Experience	27.3 years	15.5 years
Supervisory Experience	8.8 years	5.8 years
Employees Supervised	39.4 employees	28.0 employees

* The mean was used as the average.

34

University Conferences. Twenty-four of the persons enrolled in these conferences were foremen and supervisors from companies located in the community in which the conferences were presented. Their average age was 40.1 years and their education, 12.0 grades. They had averaged 15.4 years of company experience and 6.9 years of supervisory experience. Sixty-three per cent of these supervisors had attended previous human relations programs.

Comparison of the Three Types of Programs

A rather detailed description of the three different types of Human Relations Training Programs being considered in this investigation has been provided. It can be seen that the objectives, subject content, techniques and aids were similar in all programs. The principal differences concerned the length of the program, spacing of the sessions, and the instructors.

As for the supervisors attending the various programs, their characteristics were comparable with the exception of those foremen representing the Wisconsin paper mill. The supervisors from this mill were considerably older, had had more company experience, and had received less education than the other groups being studied.

The Measuring Instrument

Katzell, who is regarded as an authority in this field, specifically advocates the use of a measuring instrument which is based on the objectives of each program to be evaluated. In compliance with this recommendation, the writer searched for a test or inventory which covered the objectives of the University Institutes. Several inventories were found which contained some items that were related to the subject content of the Institutes, but none of these tests could be considered to cover all of the objectives of the programs being investigated. It was decided therefore to construct an appropriate measuring instrument.

Type of Question. Careful study and consideration were given to several different types of items. The multiple choice question, which gives three or more possible responses, was first considered. Another possibility that was studied was the open-ended or free-response type of item. Consideration was also given the dichotomous question, which results in such responses as "Yes – No" or Agree – Disagree."

The dichotomous type of question was adopted for the present study for several reasons. First of all, it is simple to understand. Also, it permits the respondents to answer the most questions in a short period of time. Finally, the responses lend themselves readily to statistical analysis.

Choice of Items. From the available measuring instruments dealing with supervisors and foremen, four were selected for further study because of their close relationship to the programs being studied. The most popular of these, HOW SUPERVISE? (9) contained thirteen items which were borrowed because they deal specifically with subject matter which is discussed in the University Institute programs. Nine other pertinent items were selected from Osterberg's SUPERVISORY INVENTORY (41). An additional eighteen items were adapted from two other sources, eleven from the SELF ANALYSIS QUIZ

(37) and seven from a test called WHAT IS YOUR MANAGEMENT I.Q? (37). (See Exhibit F for the specific items selected from each of the four inventories.) The remaining sixty items of the Inventory were drawn up by the investigator to cover the facts and principles that are discussed in each of the University Institutes.[1] In order to make sure that these one hundred items covered the objectives and subject content of the Institute programs, they were discussed with several other staff members,

The wording of each of these items was based on words and phrases used in the lectures and discussions of previous Institutes. No attempt was made to test the reading difficulty of the Inventory.

Arrangement of Items. The items so constructed were divided into two categories, one dealing with determined facts and the other covering principles only. Part one, containing twenty-nine items, was named "KNOW-WHAT," and part two, containing seventy-one items, was called "KNOW-HOW."

Items covering each subject topic were distributed throughout the test. No attempt was made to arrange items in order of difficulty.

---

[1]It should be noted that the investigator had organized, supervised, administered, and instructed in more than fifteen University Institutes before attempting to construct the Inventory. Therefore, he was thoroughly familiar with the objectives, techniques, and subject content of these programs.

Determination of Correct Responses. In order to determine the correct response to each item, the investigator administered the Inventory to the eight persons responsible for the direction, supervision, and instruction of the programs being studied. Six of these persons were staff members of the University Institutes. Dr. Russell Moberly, who conducted the program in the Wisconsin paper mill, and Dr. Milton Gordon, who did likewise in the Iowa manufacturing company, completed the group. The correct responses to each item may be found in Exhibit G.

The eight administrators agreed unanimously on eighty-seven of the items. Only one person dissented on the correct responses to ten additional items. Of the remaining three items, two persons disagreed on two items and three dissented on the remaining one. Correct answers were determined by the majority responses to each item.

Reliability. Several possibilities for determining the reliability of the Inventory were considered. The test-retest method, in which the same persons take the same test after an interval of time, was first considered. Another technique, which requires the use of alternate forms of the same test, was investigated. A third method, the split-half technique was also studied.

For this investigation, the split-half method of determining the coefficient of reliability was chosen because it has the distinct advantage of being applicable where only one test has been administered. Thus, the Inventory was divided into two parts of fifty items each on an odd-even basis as recommended by McNemar (36) and Thorndike (31). Because this odd-even split requires that the two halves be of approximately equal difficulty, the

38

total number of incorrect responses to each of the two halves were determined. The number of incorrect responses to the odd items differed from the incorrect responses to the even items by less than four per cent. It was therefore concluded that this type of split was satisfactory.

The Pearson Product-Moment formula revealed a reliability coefficient of .897. The application of the Spearman-Brown formula raised the figure to .94, the reliability coefficient of the entire Inventory. (See Exhibit H for an explanation of the use of the Pearson Product-Moment and Spearman-Brown formulas.)

In answer to the question, "How reliable should a test be?" Kelly (31) advocates the desired reliability coefficients found in Table II.

TABLE II

DESIRED TEST RELIABILITY COEFFICIENTS
FOR VARIOUS PURPOSES

Reliability Coefficient	Purpose of the Test
.50	To evaluate level of group accomplishment
.90	To evaluate differences in level of group accomplishment in two or more performances
.94	To evaluate level of individual accomplishment
.98	To evaluate differences in level of individual accomplishments in two or more performances.

From this table we can conclude that the test seems to have sufficient reliability to measure the differences between group performance on pretest and posttest.

According to Thorndike (31), other information is necessary in order to interpret reliability coefficients. In addition to a description of the technique used, he believes that consideration must be given to personal factors of the group tested, statistical characteristics of group scores, and a description of the sample.

The group used to obtain the reliability coefficient of the SUPERVISORY INVENTORY ON HUMAN RELATIONS consisted of the sixty-one foremen and supervisors who attended the first four of the six University Institutes included in this study. Their mean scores on the pretest were 80 with a standard deviation of 10.3. The sample consisted of all male persons with a mean age of 40.4 years and a mean education of 11.3 grades. This group is thus representative of the groups on which the instrument was later used.

Relevance. The question of relevance should be considered when discussing any test or inventory. Cureton (31), writing in Lindquist's book of Educational Measurement, states:

> "An ordinary subject-matter test has usually been considered to possess curricular relevance to the extent that it tests the students' knowledge and effective grasp of those facts, principles, relations, patterns, and generalizations which are the 'de facto' immediate objectives of instruction."

40

File and Remmers (10) in the manual for HOW SUPERVISE?, a paper-and-pencil inventory discussed in some detail in Chapter II and the earlier part of this chapter, go a step further when they state:

> "HOW SUPERVISE? measures understanding of general aspects of supervision. There is always the possibility that the supervisor will fail to make the best use of his knowledge. We can be sure, however, that the supervisor who does not have the knowledge will be much less likely to make the right decisions. In other words, while a supervisor may not use the knowledge he possesses, he can not use knowledge and understanding which he does not have."

The curricular relevance, or "face validity" as it is sometimes called, of the measuring instrument used in this investigation seems to be established by the fact that the items of the Inventory were based on the objectives and subject content of the programs being studied. The correct responses were determined by the eight persons who were responsible for the supervision, administration, and instruction of the programs. On eighty-seven of the items, the agreement was complete, and on ten additional items only one person dissented.

Limitations. As has been implied in the previous discussions of the improvised measuring instrument, the Inventory was designed to measure an understanding of and agreement with the subject content of the programs being studied. The items were based on the objectives of the University Institutes. The Inventory was also used to evaluate the effectiveness of the Company Programs. Although the objectives and subject content were similar to the University Institutes, it is possible that certain facts and principles were not even mentioned in one or both of the Company Programs. This was due mainly to the shorter length of these programs.

Another important consideration is the fact that the results of this evaluation must not be taken as a final indication of the value of the programs. This study is aimed at determining the effectiveness with which the subject matter was understood and accepted by the foremen as revealed on the SUPERVISORY INVENTORY ON HUMAN RELATIONS. There was no attempt to determine other benefits that the foremen might have received. They may have gone back to their jobs with a realization that they are working for an outstanding company, with new insight into their job, with new enthusiasm to develop themselves as better foremen, with a feeling that the company considers them very important management persons, with one or more ideas they picked up from other foremen, or with an answer to a problem that had been bothering them for a long time.

An important consideration concerning the acceptance of facts and principles by the foremen attending the programs is the human relations "climate" surrounding the plant jobs from which the foremen came. This was one of the conclusions of the study conducted by the Survey Research Center of the University of Michigan (32). If, for example, a foreman had a boss who liked to see his subordinates "drive" the men instead of "lead" them, the foreman may not be as receptive to leadership techniques as a foreman whose boss encouraged more acceptable human relations tactics. This conclusion was reached by Fleishman (11) in his recent doctoral dissertation.

There are present, of course, those limitations that apply
to any paper-and-pencil inventory. There is no assurance
that supervisors answered all of the items in accordance
with their behavior on the job. What they said and what
they did when they returned to their jobs may have been
inconsistent.

Methods of Treating the Five Problems Involved in This Study

The objectives, subject content, and techniques of the
human relations training programs involved in this
investigation were discussed in detail at the beginning of
this chapter. The measuring instrument was also treated at
some length. With this background material in mind, the
specific methods and techniques for analyzing the data and
dealing with the problems will now be described. Each of
the five questions involved in this investigation was
considered separately.

1. How Effective Are Human Relations Programs in Imparting Knowledge and Changing Attitudes of Industrial Foremen and Supervisors?

Each of the six University Institutes, the two series of
University Conferences, the program in the Wisconsin paper
mill, and the program in the Iowa manufacturing company
were treated as separate units in order to evaluate their
effectiveness. The same methods and procedures were
followed in each case.

Comment sheets of the trainees provided the first
indication of the effectiveness of the programs. (Exhibit
I contains a University Institute comment sheet.) Although

these sheets included specific ratings for each of the instructors appearing on the program, their tabulation gives more of an indication of how much the program was enjoyed than of the knowledge gained or the attitudes changed.

A comparison of pretest scores with posttest scores for each foreman revealed the gain in Inventory scores. The average gain for each program was tabulated and from this information the "t" scores were computed. (See Exhibit J for an explanation of the computation of "t.") By using a "t" table, the probability of the gain having occurred as a result of chance was determined. If the probability was found to be .001, for example, the conclusion would have been drawn that only one time in a thousand would the gain have resulted from chance. It would be almost certain, then, that the gain could be attributed to the program. If, however, the probability was found to be .10, the conclusion would have been made that the gain was so small that it would appear as a result of chance one time in ten. It would be questionable, in this latter case, if the gain could be attributed to the program rather than to chance alone.

A third indication of the effectiveness of the program was found by analyzing each item. Chi square was used to determine which items showed significant change from pretest to posttest. The following formula, advocated by McNemar (36:206), was used:

44

$$X^2 = \frac{(A - D)^2}{A + D}$$

in which:

    x^2 = chi square

    A = changes from "Agree" on pretest to "Disagree" on posttest

    D = changes from "Disagree" on pretest to "Agree" on posttest.

In case A + D totaled less than 10, the following formula was applied:

$$X^2 = \frac{[(A - D) - 1]^2}{A + D}$$

In accordance with customary practice, items showing changes at the .05 level (can be attributed to chance only one time in twenty) were considered to be significant.

Analyses, then, of comment sheets, gains from pretest to posttest on the SUPERVISORY INVENTORY ON HUMAN RELATIONS, and Inventory items showing changes significant at the .05 level provide answers to the first problem which deals with the effectiveness of the programs being studied.

2. How Valid is the SUPERVISORY INVENTORY ON HUMAN RELATIONS as a Measure of Job Performance?

It was decided that the best method to answer this question was to compare Inventory responses with on-the-job performance. The simplest acceptable method to make this comparison was to rank the foremen from best to poorest on the basis of job performance and to compare these rankings with Inventory scores.

The foremen and supervisors who attended the University programs represented many varied companies. Therefore, it did not seem practical to attempt to rank them. In each of the two private companies, however, it did seem feasible to rank the foremen. The following procedures were used in the ranking process.

Performance Ranking of Supervisors. The two companies were treated separately in the ranking process. In the Iowa manufacturing company, a rating of the foremen was already available. This rating had been made approximately one month prior to the completion of the Human Relations Training Program for the purpose of giving out merit bonuses. The following procedure had been used in making the rating.

Four Merit Committee Members, consisting of the Assistant General Manager, General Superintendent, Personnel Manager, and Employment Manager rated each supervisor. The Merit Rating From, described in Exhibit E, was used. These ratings were independently made by the four committee members, and a total point score was given each supervisor by each rater. Each supervisor's four scores were added together and the mean was computed. This figure was considered to be the final rating score for each supervisor. This rating seemed adaptable for this study. Therefore, the supervisors were ranked in order, from best to poorest, on the basis of their final rating score.

In the Wisconsin paper mill, however, a rating of the foreman was not available. It was necessary, therefore, to devise a system of ranking the foremen on the basis of their job performance. A rating technique described in detail by Jennings (18) was adopted for this study.

Five management persons seemed qualified to compare the job performances of all of the supervisors in the company. These five, selected as the Ranking Committee, consisted of the Vice President of Manufacturing, Manager of Manufacturing, Personnel Director, Employment Manager, and Training Director. Because it seemed difficult to rank thirty-six foremen in order, they were randomly divided into four groups of nine each. The ranking committee independently ranked these four groups using the ranking form shown in Exhibit L.

A correlation of these rankings by the Pearson Product-Moment method revealed the matrix shown in Table III.

TABLE III

A STUDY OF THE CORRELATION OF THE
RANKING BY FIVE MANAGEMENT REPRESENTATIVES

Ranker No.	1	2	3	4	5
1		.87	.52	.65	.19
2	.87		.56	.63	.24
3	.52	.56		.64	.51
4	.65	.63	.64		.33
5	.19	.24	.51	.33	

In testing for the possibility of the rankers agreeing because of chance, intercorrelations must be +.36 to be significant at the .05 level (56:424). This means that if correlation coefficients of less than +.36 are used, the chances are more than one in twenty that chance alone accounts for the similarity between the rankings. Because three of the correlations between Ranker No. 5 and the other rankers were less than the desired +.36, the rankings of No. 5 were not used. Since this ranker was the youngest in both age and length of company service, and because he had had the least contact with the job performances of the men, the discarding of his rankings seemed valid.

By converting the rankings made by each of the remaining four committee members to a five point scale (Exhibit N), the individual rankings were combined into an overall ranking. Thus, the supervisors in the Wisconsin paper mill were ranked from best to poorest on the basis of their job performance. The final rankings included only thirty foremen, because the remaining six were not ranked by one or more of the four committee members.

Comparison of Rankings with Inventory Scores. An analysis was made of the relationship of test scores to the on-the-job performance of the supervisors for each of the companies separately. By means of the rank-difference method as described in McNemar (36:97), an easily computed correlation (rho) was obtained. (See Exhibit N for a description of the use of the rank-difference formula.) The procedure compared the foremen's ranks on the pretest with their ranks as determined by on-the-job performance. The resulting rho compares very favorably with the customary r, according to Guilford (14). He states: "....and in no case is the difference between rho and r greater than .018, and in every case except for coefficients of zero or 1.00, r is greater than rho."

The coefficient of correlation between the ranks of foremen on the basis of on-the-job performance and their ranks on the basis of pretest scores answers the second problem which concerns the validity of the test in measuring job performance.

3. Which Items of the Inventory Can Be Used in the Selection of Supervisors?

One of the problems faced by the management personnel of nearly all companies today is the selection of persons who will become good supervisors. Problem 3 attempts to see if certain items on the Inventory used in this investigation discriminate between "good" and "poor" supervisors.

The foremen in the two private companies included in the present study were ranked from best to poorest as described earlier in this Chapter. Because the number of supervisors included in the final rankings was small (thirty in the Wisconsin company and twenty-eight in the Iowa company), it was decided to consider the upper half as "good" supervisors and the lower half as "poor" supervisors. In each company separately, the number of "good" supervisors who got each item correct on the pretest was compared with the number of "poor" ones who had the right answer. The same procedure was followed for the number from each group who got each item wrong. The preparation of a fourfold contingency table and the application of chi square determined the power of each item to discriminate between "good" and "poor" foremen. (See Exhibit O for the construction of the contingency table and the use of the chi square formula.)

It can be concluded that the items discriminating between "good" and "poor" supervisors in each company will be items which should prove useful in the selection of supervisors for that company. In order to properly use these items in another company, however, their ability to discriminate between "good" and "poor" supervisors in that particular company would have to be proven.

4. Which Foremen Seem to Benefit Most from the Human Relations Training?

The gain on Inventory scores from pretest to posttest was used as the measure of the benefit that was derived. An attempt was made to determine whether there was a relationship between the amount of gain and the personal characteristics of the foremen. It seemed important to find out, for example, whether the best educated supervisors showed the largest gains. It would be interesting and valuable to know also, if the supervisors with more experience showed high gains than the new foremen. With information like this, foremen who would benefit most could be selected for training while others would not receive the training.

In order to discover if any relationships existed, the gains on Inventory scores were correlated with six different characteristics of the foremen, namely: age, education, company experience, supervisory experience, number of employees supervised, and on-the-job performance. This was done for the supervisors in the two companies where all of the data were available by using rank-difference correlation procedures.

5. <u>What Subject Matter Should Be Stressed in Future University Institutes</u>?

In order to improve the quality of the University Institutes, the program should be related to the needs of the foremen and supervisors who attend. This might be done by determining the knowledges and attitudes which supervisors bring to the program.

A tabulation was made of the incorrect responses to each item of the Inventory by the eighty-four foremen and supervisors who attended the six Institutes involved in the present study. The per cent of incorrect responses to each item was then computed. (See Exhibit P.) From these data, an indication was obtained of subject topics which need to be stressed in future programs.

<u>Chapter Summary</u>

This investigation is concerned with five specific problems.

1. How Effective Are Human Relations Programs in Imparting Facts and Principles to Industrial Foremen and Supervisors?
2. How Valid is the SUPERVISORY INVENTORY ON HUMAN RELATIONS as a Measure of Job Performance?
3. Which Items of the Inventory Can Be Used in the Selection of Supervisors?
4. Which Foremen Seem to Benefit Most from Human Relations Training?
5. What Subject Matter Should Be Stressed in Future University Institutes?

In order to attack the first and main problem of the present study, a measuring instrument called the SUPERVISORY INVENTORY ON HUMAN RELATIONS was constructed. A comparison of pretest and posttest responses was made to indicate the effectiveness of the programs. The comment sheets of the enrollees were used as an additional evaluative device.

Scores on the pretest were correlated with the on-the-job performance of the foremen in two private companies to solve problem 2. These foremen had been ranked from best to poorest on the basis of performance on their jobs. A correlation of the ranking on pretest scores with the ranking on performance was used to determine the validity of the Inventory to measure job performance.

Reponses to each item on the inventory were tested against "good" and "poor" supervision. The items discriminating between the two classes of supervisors may be considered to be valid in the selection of new supervisors in the respective companies, thereby answering the third problem.

Gains on the Inventory from pretest to posttest were correlated with age, education, company experience, supervisory experience, number of employees supervised, and performance on the job. The closeness of these relationships indicates which foremen benefited most from human relations training.

Finally, the incorrect responses to each item on the inventory were tabulated for the foremen attending the six University Institutes being studied. Items showing the highest per cent of incorrect responses can be considered to be good indications of subject matter which should be stressed in future University Institutes.

CHAPTER IV

FINDINGS AND INTERPRETATIONS

How Effective Are Human Relations Programs?

The primary purpose of this study was to evaluate the effectiveness of several different programs in human relations. Consequently, most of the time and effort of the investigator was spent in answering this question, the first of the five included in the scope of this study.

University Institute, January 12-16, 1953. The first indication of the success of this program came from an analysis of enrollee comment sheets. (An Institute comment sheet is included in Exhibit I.) Every enrollee rated each discussion leader as having been "excellent," "good," "fair," or "poor." A summation of all of the ratings for the Institute revealed the following:

Excellent	Good	Fair	Poor
89	64	9	2

By assigning point values to the four possible ratings (excellent = 4, good = 3, etc.), an average point value for the entire Institute was computed. It was found to be 3.46 which indicated an average rating of approximately halfway between "excellent" and "good." In other words, the Institute was well received by those in attendance.

Table IV shows the results of the pretesting and posttesting of the twenty-two foremen attending this Institute. The SUPERVISRY INVENTORY ON HUMAN RELATIONS was used as the measuring instrument.

TABLE IV

INVENTORY SCORES FOR THE TWENTY-TWO SUPERVISORS
ATTENDING THE UNIVERSITY INSTITUTE,
JANUARY 12-16, 1953

	Pretest	Posttest	Gain
Mean	79.8	84.8	5.0
Standard Deviation	7.3	7.6	3.3
Range	62-91	71-95	(1)-11

Table IV reveals an average gain of 5.0 with a S.D. of 3.3. In order to determine whether this was a significant gain or if it probably occurred because of chance alone, the "t" ratio was computed. (See Exhibit J for the computation.) This was found to be 6.9. Reference to a "t" table (36:368) revealed a probability (P) of less than .001. This means that a gain as large as 5.0 would occur by chance less than one time in one thousand. It is almost certain, then, that attendance and participation in the Insttitute resulted in increased knowledge.

A third approach to the evaluation of this Institute concerned each Inventory item. For the determination of the responses to which items changed significantly from pretest to posttest, a chi square formula was used. (See

Chapter III.)   Three items were found that showed changes significant at the .05 level (could be attributed to chance only one time in twenty.)   These items were the following:

Item No.		Changed From
28.	The person with the highest intelligence, best personality and most experience should always be selected for a job.	"A" to "DA"
56.	A supervisor should accept and carry out any order he receives from an important representative of another department.	"A" to "DA"
75.	A knowledge of learning curves and plateaus is important to a supervisor.	"DA" to "A"

From these three analyses of the effectiveness of this Institute (comment sheets, changes in total score, change on each item), it can be concluded that the enrollees were highly satisfied with the program and benefited from it in the form of increased knowledge of human relations facts and principles.   The fact that only three items showed significant change indicates that different foremen and supervisors learned and accepted different facts and principles.

University Institute, February 23-27, 1953. A summary of
the comment sheets of this Institute revealed the
following:

Excellent	Good	Fair	Poor	Average Rating
55	62	6	0	3.4

Responses to the Inventory are shown in Table V.

TABLE V

INVENTORY SCORES FOR THE TEN SUPERVISORS
ATTENDING THE UNIVERSITY INSTITUTE,
FEBRUARY 23-27, 1953

	Pretest	Posttest	Gain
Mean	80.5	88.3	7.8
S.D.	5.8	5.7	4.5
Range	72-92	79-97	②-14

The interpretation of the gain revealed a "t" score of 5.2.
Reference to the "t" table showed that the probability of
this gain having occurred because of chance was less than
.001.

In analyzing each item, it was found that only item number
28 showed a change significant at the .05 level. This item
was changed from "Agree" to "Disagree." The item stated:
The person with the highest intelligence, best personality
and most experience should always be selected for a job.

The findings in regard to this Institute reveal that the enrollees were well satisfied with the program. The analysis of responses to the inventory clearly indicates that the knowledges of the foremen were increased as a result of their attendance.

University Institute, March 16-20, 1953. The comment sheets of the enrollees of this program were summarized and revealed the following distribution:

Excellent	Good	Fair	Poor	Average Rating
74	55	5	1	3.5

Inventory responses are show in Table VI.

TABLE VI

INVENTORY SCORES OF THE FIFTEEN SUPERVISORS
ATTENDING THE UNIVERSITY INSTITUTE,
MARCH 16-20, 1953

	Pretest	Posttest	Gain
Mean	80.6	83.9	3.3
S.D.	13.2	12.1	7.1
Range	55-92	47-93	⑧-23

The "t" score for the gain on this Institute was found to be 1.7 with a probability greater than .1. This means that more than one time in ten, a gain of 3.3 could result from chance alone. It is doubtful, then, whether any gain in knowledge can be attributed to the Institute.

An item analysis revealed that no items showed changes significant at the .05 level of confidence.

This Institute, then, seems to have been enjoyed by the participants. However, little evidence of increased knowledge was found.

University Institute, April 6-10, 1953. The summary of comment sheets showed the following:

Excellent	Good	Fair	Poor	Average Rating
59	46	6	1	3.5

A tabulation of responses to the inventory are described in Table VII.

TABLE VII

INVENTORY SCORES FOR THE FOURTEEN SUPERVISORS
ATTENDING THE UNIVERSITY INSTITUTE,
APRIL 6-10, 1953

	Pretest	Posttest	Gain
Mean	77.1	82.7	5.6
S.D.	12.4	11.5	3.7
Range	45-96	51-99	③-13

The computation of "t" revealed a value of 5.6. Reference to a "t" table indicated a probability of .001.

An item analysis revealed that item number 7 was the only one which changed significantly. The change was from "Agree" to "Disagree." The item stated: Intelligence consists of what we've learned since we were born.

Both the comment sheets and the analysis of Inventory responses showed that this Institute was effective. The enrollees themselves rated it as being "very good" and the size of the gains from pretest to posttest clearly indicates that facts and principles were learned and accepted by the foremen.

University Institute, April 27-May 1, 1953. The tabulation of the comment sheets revealed the following:

Excellent	Good	Fair	Poor	Average Rating
39	37	14	0	3.28

The scores on the Inventory are described in Table VIII.

TABLE VIII

INVENTORY SCORES FOR THE TWELVE SUPERVISORS
ATTENDING THE UNIVERSITY INSTITUTE,
APRIL 27-May 1, 1953

	Pretest	Posttest	Gain
Mean	76.5	81.5	5.0
S.D.	8.8	10.0	5.7
Range	60-92	57-95	(6)-14

The "t" score was found to be 2.9 which translated to a probability of .02. No items were found to show changes which were significant at the .05 level.

The findings in regard to this Institute reveal that the enrollees considered the program to be slightly better than "good." An analysis of Inventory responses indicated that the foremen did benefit in the form of increased knowledge.

University Institute, May 26-30, 1953. To find out whether Institute staff members were better instructors than discussion leaders selected from business and industry, all of the sessions in this Institute were handled by the staff. The comment sheets revealed the following reaction:

Excellent	Good	Fair	Poor	Average Rating
65	56	4	0	3.5

The responses to the Inventory are described in Table IX.

TABLE IX

INVENTORY SCORES FOR THE ELEVEN SUPERVISORS
ATTENDING THE UNIVERSITY INSTITUTE,
May 26-30, 1953

	Pretest	Posttest	Gain
Mean	79.8	88.1	8.3
S.D.	7.3	5.5	2.7
Range	69-95	78-98	3-12

The "t" score was found to be 9.8, the highest found for any of the six Institutes. The probability was much less than .001.

Only item number 82 was found to have changed significantly from pretest to posttest. The change was from "Agree" to Disagree." The item read: The best way to train a new worker is to have him watch a good worker at the job.

The comment sheets revealed the same high level of satisfaction that was found on the other Institutes. The analysis of the pretest and posttest responses on the Inventory showed that this Institute was effective in teaching facts and principles. The average gain in scores from pretest to posttest of 8.3 points was found to be highly significant. Different foremen learned a variety of facts and principles as evidenced by the fact that only one item showed significant change from pretest to posttest. Since this Institute was the only one conducted entirely by University staff personnel, an inference can be drawn that staff instructors seem to be at least as effective as business and industrial leaders in teaching human relations facts and principles.

Company Program, Wisconsin Paper Mill. The comment sheets revealed a high degree of satisfaction with the program as evidenced by Table X.

TABLE X

SUMMARY OF TRAINEE REACTIONS TO THE HUMAN
RELATIONS PROGRAM CONDUCTED AT THE WISCONSIN PAPER MILL

SUBJECT MATTER	61%	39%	0%
	of great value	O.K.	of little value

GROUP DISCUSSION	5%	80%	15%
	too much	just right	not enough

ATTITUDE OF DIS-CUSSION LEADER	80%	20%	0%
	open-minded	O.K.	too opinionated

RESULTS OF PROGRAM	1%	54%	45%
	did me no good	O.K. but should have more	made me a better supervisor

The second indication of program effectiveness is illustrated is Table XI.

TABLE XI

INVENTORY SCORES FOR THE THIRTY-FOUR SUPERVISORS
FROM THE WISCONSIN PAPER MILL

	Pretest	Posttest	Gain
Mean	77.5	79.9	2.4
S.D.	9.9	9.7	5.1
Range	41-91	48-95	⑥-17

The "t" score was found to be 2.73 for the thirty-four foremen involved. Reference to the "t" table revealed a probability of .01 which indicated clearly that a significant gain had taken place in test scores.

It was discovered by analyzing each item that items number 41 and 58 changed significantly from pretest to posttest. The responses to both items changed from "Agree" to "Disagree." The items were:

41. A good supervisor must be able to do all the jobs performed by the workers he supervises.

58. Asking the worker to criticise his own work will do more harm than good.

From the comment sheets and the comparison of posttest scores with pretest scores the conclusion can be drawn that the program was enjoyed by the foremen and was effective in teaching facts and principles. Since only two items changed significantly from pretest to posttest, the interpretation can be made that different foremen learned different things from the course.

Company Program, Iowa Manufacturing Company. A tabulation of the comment sheets of the trainees revealed the following:

Excellent	Good	Fair	Poor	Average Rating
17	11	1	1	3.5

A comparison of pretest scores with posttest scores on the Inventory are included in Table XII.

TABLE XII

INVENTORY SCORES FOR THE THIRTY SUPERVISORS FROM
THE IOWA MANUFACTURING COMPANY

	Pretest	Posttest	Gain
Mean	78.1	80.5	2.4
S.D.	7.4	8.9	4.2
Range	56-92	56-96	6-10

The "t" score was calculated and found to be 3.2. The probability was .01. This indicated that it is almost certain that the gain in test scores resulted from attendance and participation rather than from chance alone.

An item analysis was made to see which items had changed significantly from pretest to posttest. The responses to four items showed significant changes. The items showing changes along with the direction of the change follow:

Item No.		Direction of Change
28.	The person with the highest intelligence, best personality and most experience should always be selected for a job.	"A" to "DA"

39.   The well-trained working   "DA" to "A"
        force is a result of
        maintaining a large training
        department.

75.   A knowledge of learning   "DA" to "A"
        curves and plateaus is
        important to a supervisor.

96.   The training needs of a   "DA" to "A"
        department should be
        determined by the supervisor
        in charge.

Since the correct answer to item 39 is "DA," it is interesting to note that the change was not in the desired direction. This is the only evidence in the entire investigation of an item changing significantly in the wrong direction.

The evidence seems to be quite conclusive that the Human Relations Program in the Iowa company was effective. The analyses of pretest and posttest responses to the inventory reveal gains that were found to be significant at the .01 level.

University Conferences, Milwaukee. A summary of comment sheets revealed the following distribution:

| | | | | Average |
Excellent	Good	Fair	Poor	Rating
56	46	0	0	3.55

This reaction indicated that the program was very well received by the enrollees.

The comparison of Inventory scores on pretest and posttest is shown in Table XIII.

"T" was computed as 2.73 which corresponded to a probability of .02. Item analysis revealed no items which changed significantly from pretest to posttest.

TABLE XIII

INVENTORY SCORES FOR THE ELEVEN SUPERVISORS
ATTENDING THE MILWAUKEE UNIVERSITY CONFERENCES

	Pretest	Posttest	Gain
Mean	83.5	87.6	4.1
S.D.	7.4	6.0	4.9
Range	73-92	79-97	③-10

The reaction to this series of four one-day conferences was very favorable. Also, the analysis of responses to the Inventory gave a clear indication that a gain in understanding of facts and principles had taken place during the course of the program.

University Conferences, Racine. The comment sheets were summarized as follows:

Excellent	Good	Fair	Poor	Average Rating
67	36	1	2	3.59

The reaction to this program, as revealed by the tabulation of comment sheets, was more favorable than any of the other programs involved in the study.

Table XIV includes the comparison of pretest and posttest responses to the Inventory.

The "t" score was found to be 4.7 which corresponded to a probability of .001. An analysis of items revealed none which changed significantly from pretest to posttest.

TABLE XIV

INVENTORY SCORES FOR THE THIRTEEN SUPERVISORS
ATTENDING THE RACINE UNIVERSITY CONFERENCES

	Pretest	Posttest	Gain
Mean	83.2	87.3	4.1
S.D.	7.0	6.1	3.1
Range	68-93	73-96	(1)-10

The evidence clearly indicates a high degree of satisfaction with the program as well as an improvement in the knowledges of the foremen who attended the program.

How Valid is the SUPERVISORY INVENTORY ON HUMAN RELATIONS As a Measure of Job Performance?

The Inventory was designed to measure the changes in understanding and acceptance of the subject matter of the Human Relations Programs being considered in this investigation. (The reliability and relevance of the instrument were described in detail in Chapter III.) It was therefore used to determine whether these immediate objectives of the programs were reached.

The real purpose of the training, however, was to improve the supervisory performance of the foremen attending the sessions. The understanding, acceptance, and application of the subject matter by the supervisors, it was hoped, would raise the morale of the workers and increase the quality and quantity of production. It therefore seems necessary to see whether the Inventory actually measures performance on the job. In other words, do the understanding and acceptance of the subject matter mean better supervisory performance?

The foremen in the two private companies were ranked from best to poorest on the basis of their job performance. (Details of the ranking procedures were given in Chapter III.) The pretest scores of these foremen were compared with their performance ranking to see whether high test scores indicated a high level of job performance.

The rank-difference method was used to determine the correlation between pretest scores on the Inventory and performance on the job. (Details on the use of rank-difference correlation can be found in Exhibit N.) In the Wisconsin paper mill, the correlation (rho) was found to be +.35. This corresponds to a .06 level of significance (56:424). The conclusion can therefore be drawn that the better supervisors had a definite tendency to obtain higher scores on the Inventory.

In the Iowa manufacturing company, the same method was used to compute the relationship between Inventory scores and job performance. The correlation between the two was found to be -.15. This indicates that the better supervisors tended to have lower scores on the Inventory, although this negative relationship was not significant.

Assuming that the rankings of the foremen were valid, it can be concluded that high scores on the pretest indicated a high level of job performance in one company. In this company, the relationship was significant at the .06 level. In the other company, however, an insignificant negative correlation was discovered.

Several possible explanations might be made for the lack of a significant positive correlation in the latter company. First of all, there is the possibility that the poorer supervisors knew the correct responses to many of the items but did not make use of the facts and principles on the job. Another possible explanation is the fact that the performance rankings of the foremen might have been weighted toward the technical aspects of the job rather than the human relations aspects of the job. If the rankers were more concerned with a knowledge of the job than with the ability to get along with the workers, the ratings would be biased in favor of foremen who had a thorough knowledge of all the work they supervise. Consequently, scores on this human relations inventory would not be a measure of job performance.

The wording of the Inventory items may be another explanation of the lack of a significant positive relationship between Inventory scores and job performance. If the test correlates highly with intelligence, education, or similar factors, it would probably not be a good measure

70

of performance on the job, especially for those foremen who are lowest on the factors with which the test correlates.

A final possibility is that the subject matter which was taught in the program is not related to success on the job. Perhaps the foremen who know these basic human relations facts and principles are no better at performing their supervisory duties than those who do not understand them.

Any or all of these four possible explanations' may have caused the absence of a correlation between Inventory scores and on-the-job performance in the Iowa manufacturing company. Only through further research can the real explanation be found.

Which Items of the Inventory Can Be Used in the Selection of Supervisor?

In order to determine which items would be valid as a device for selecting supervisors, the ranked foremen in each company were divided into two groups, an upper half and a lower half. Thus, for each company, a group was formed which could be classified as "good" supervisors and a group that could be classified as "poor" supervisors.

The responses to each item on the Inventory were then tabulated for each of the groups separately. On each item was determined the number of "good" supervisors who answered it correctly and the number of "good" supervisors who answered it incorrectly. The same procedure was followed in tabulating the responses of the "poor" foremen.

Through the use of the fourfold contingency table and the chi square formula (see Exhibit O for details), the power of each item to discriminate between "good" and "poor" foremen was determined. This was computed for each of the companies separately.

In the Wisconsin paper mill, four items were found which discriminated between "good" and "poor" supervisors at the .06 level of confidence (could be attributed to chance less than one time in sixteen). These items were:

Item No.		Level of Significance
41.	A good supervisor must be able to do all the jobs performed by the workers he supervises.	.02
51.	The more details a supervisor handles by himself, the better executive he is likely to be.	.06
64.	The personnel department or training department should be responsible to see that training is done in all departments.	.05
82.	The best way to train a new worker is to have him watch a good worker at the job.	.01

In the Iowa manufacturing company, one significant item was found which discriminated at the .02 level (could be attributed to chance less than once in fifty times.) This item was number 59 and reads: A good instruction rule is to emphasize how _not_ to do the job.

This difference between the items that discriminated in one case and did not discriminate in another case can be interpreted in several ways. First of all, the ranking procedure, which led to the division of "good" and "poor" supervisors, was different in the two plants. Also, since this ranking was based on the judgments of others, it is subject to the bias and subjective pitfalls that might be associated with any judgment criteria.

It is well accepted that any test must be validated in the situation in which it is used. Therefore, the four items which discriminate between "good" and "poor" foremen in the Wisconsin paper mill might not be valid items in any other company. Plant conditions vary from one company to another so greatly that the characteristics of a good foreman in one plant are probably different from the characteristics of a good foreman in another plant.

The conclusion can be drawn that four items of the Inventory differentiate between "good" and "poor" supervisors in the Wisconsin paper mill. If it can be assumed that the ranking was valid, then the four items can be used as a device in selecting new supervisors. In the Iowa company, one item can be used for selecting new foremen.

From a practical standpoint, a test consisting of four or less items is probably not a good test. Therefore, these items could be included in a larger test. The responses to the valid items could then by analyzed as an indication of whether or not the applicant would become a good supervisor.

Which Foremen Seem to Benefit Most from Human Relations Programs?

The foremen who attended the two company programs were studied to answer this question. Their gains on the Inventory score from pretest to posttest were correlated with age, education, company experience, supervisory experience, employees supervised, and on-the-job performance. The rank-difference method of correlation (See Exhibit N) was used to determine all of the relationships except the correlation between gain and education. The Pearson Product-Moment formula (Exhibit H) was used in this case, because the education factor did not lend itself to rank order. Table XV shows all of the correlations.

TABLE XV

CORRELATIONS BETWEEN GAIN IN INVENTORY SCORES FROM PRETEST
TO POSTTEST AND OTHER FACTORS FOR FOREMEN FROM
TWO PRIVATE COMPANIES

	Wisconsin Paper Mill	Iowa Mfg. Company
Age.........................	.00	−.26
Education..................	−.05	+.15
Company Experience........	−.22	.00
Supervisory Experience.....	−.20	−.10
No. of Employees Supervised	−.48	.00
On-the-Job-Performance.....	−.07	−.20

Relationship between Gain and Age.   In the Wisconsin paper
mill, the correlation was found to be 0.0.   In the Iowa
company the relationship was -.26, which indicates a slight
tendency for the younger foremen to have learned more from
the program than the older ones.   The correlation is not
significant at the .05 level, however.

Relationship between Gain and Education.   A correlation of
-.05 was found in the Wisconsin company which indicates no
relationship.   In the Iowa company, the two factors
correlated +.15.   This can be interpreted as a very slight
tendency for the better educated foremen to have shown more
gain on inventory scores.   However, the relationship was
too small to be significant.

Relationship between Gain and Company Experience.   In the
Wisconsin paper mill, the correlation was found to be -.22
which indicates a slight tendency for the foremen with the
fewest years of company experience to have shown the
greatest gain.   In the Iowa company, the correlation was
exactly 0.0.

Relationship between Gain and Supervisory Experience.   In
the Wisconsin company these two factors correlated at -.20.
This can be interpreted to mean that the newer foremen
showed a little more gain than the more experienced ones.
In the Iowa company, a relationship of -.10 was discovered.
Neither of these relationships is significant.

Relationship between Gain and Number of Employees
Supervised.   In the Wisconsin paper mill, the correlation
was found to be -.48.   This indicates a definite tendency
for the foremen with fewer subordinates to have gained more

from the program. In the Iowa company the relationship was found to be 0.0.

A possible explanation of the -.48 correlation is that the foremen with fewer subordinates felt that human relations principles would be more applicable in their departments. Consequently, they were more receptive to the program and benefited more from it.

Relationship between Gain and On-the-Job Performance. The correlation for the Wisconsin company was found to be -.07 which means no relationship existed. In the Iowa company, the correlation of -.20 shows a slight tendency for the poorer foremen to have gained more from the program. This correlation (-.20) is not large enough, however, to be significant.

An examination of the six relationships just described reveals that the only significant one is the correlation between the gain from pretest to posttest and the number of employees supervised by the foremen of the Wisconsin paper mill. Since this significant relationship existed in only one of the two companies, no general interpretations can be made. This points out the fact that investigations concerned with the effectiveness of human relations training should be made for each program separately, and that it is a mistake to generalize from the results of a single study.

In answer to the question "Which Foremen Seem to Benefit Most From Human Relations Training?", the statement must be made that there seems to be no pattern. The only indication that can be drawn from this study is that in one of the two programs investigated, the foremen supervising the fewest employees derive the most benefit.

What Subject Matter Should be Stressed in Future University Institutes?

In answering this question, an assumption was made that the foremen and supervisors attending the six Institutes being studied are typical of the ones who will attend future programs. There are several factors which seem to make this assumption tenable. First of all, the Institute program will continue to attract the same level of management persons from industry. The publicity will probably include the mailing of bulletins describing the program as well as personal visits to management persons in Wisconsin industry. This same procedure has been followed for past Institutes.

Also, there are a number of companies who have adopted the policy of sending all of their foremen to the Institutes, two or three at a time. In the six University Institutes being studied, nearly all of the eighty-four foremen came from companies which, from all indications, will send additional supervisors to future Institutes. The order in which these companies send their foremen is usually decided on the basis of such factors as plant schedules, seniority, or desires of the foremen and not on the basis of ability or job performance. Therefore, there is no reason to believe that in future Institutes the representatives of these companies will be significantly different from the ones who have attended in the past.

The fact that the average scores on the pretest for the six Institutes showed a range of only 4.1 points (76.5 to 80.6) seems to be a further indication of the validity of the assumption. The inference can be drawn that there seems to be little variation in the human relations knowledges and understandings of foremen attending different Institutes.

Based on the assumption described and defended above, the responses to each item on the Inventory were tabulated for the eighty-four foremen and supervisors attending the six Institutes involved in this investigation. The mean per cent of incorrect responses was found to be 21.0 with a standard deviation of 20.1. The range is 0-80 per cent.

Table XVI lists the items which were missed by more than half of the foremen. The correct answer to all of these items is "Disagree."

The thirteen items most frequently missed by supervisors attending the University Institutes are listed in order in Table XVI. These items are indicative of the lack of knowledges and understandings that foremen bring to the University Institutes. Therefore, they should provide evidence of the needs of the supervisors who will attend future Institutes.

In the past, instructors in these University programs have had no real indication of the knowledges and facts that foremen bring to the Institutes. Various phases of the subject content have been stressed by discussion leaders because they felt it was most important. This study has proved that certain facts being discussed in the program are known by almost every foremen before the sessions begin. (See Exhibit P for the per cent of foremen who missed each of the one hundred items.)

TABLE XVI

INCORRECT RESPONSES TO ITEMS ON THE INVENTORY BY THE
EIGHTY-FOUR FOREMEN ATTENDING SIX UNIVERSITY INSTITUTES

Item No.		% Incorrect Responses
54.	In training a worker, the first thing the supervisor should do is show in detail how the job is performed.	80
7.	Intelligence consists of what we've learned since we were born.	77
70.	A worker of average intelligence should be able to do a job after he is told and shown how it should be done.	70
82.	The best way to train a new worker is to have him watch a good worker at the job.	68
18.	If we know a worker well, we can always tell what he'll do in a given situation.	68
1.	Anyone is able to do almost any job if he tries hard enough.	63
20.	Attitudes are usually based on a careful study of the facts.	58
71.	If we have an efficient, intelligent, ambitious, and likeable worker in our department, we should do everything we can to keep him there.	58
39.	The well-trained working force is a result of maintaining a large training department.	54

10.	If a supervisor knows all about the work to be done, he is therefore qualified to teach a worker how to do it.	51
12.	Everyone is either an introvert or an extrovert.	51
25.	The best way to overcome frustrations is to fight vigorously.	51
56.	A supervisor should accept and carry out any order he receives from an important representative of another department.	51

In future Institutes, each discussion leader will have a good indication of subject content which can be virtually ignored because it is understood by most of the foremen in attendance. At the same time, he can determine which topics should be clarified and stressed in order to meet the needs of the enrollees. Through the emphasizing of human relations facts and principles with which the majority of foremen disagree, the University Institutes can be made more effective.

CHAPTER V

SUMMARY, CONCLUSIONS, AND RECOMMENDATIONS

Summary

The primary purpose of this study has been centered in an attempt to evaluate the effectiveness of several selected programs on human relations for industrial foremen and supervisors. The Industrial Management Institute of the University of Wisconsin served as the main laboratory in which the investigation was made. In addition, two private companies, one in Wisconsin and the other in Iowa, provided an opportunity for comparative evaluations.

As recommended by authorities and practitioners, it was decided to use a paper-and-pencil inventory as a measure of the effectiveness of the programs. The SUPERVISORY INVENTORY ON HUMAN RELATIONS used in this study, was constructed to cover the specific objectives and subject content of the University of Wisconsin Institutes. A comparison of pretest and posttest scores was made to determine whether the knowledges of the foremen had changed significantly as a result of attendance and participation in the program. This means of comparison was used as the principal indication of program effectiveness.

Ten different human relations programs were evaluated in this manner. They included eight that were sponsored by the University of Wisconsin and two that were conducted in private companies.

All ten of these programs were well received by the
trainees. The comment sheets which were filled out by
enrollees at the conclusion of each program consistently
rated the instructors and subject content as being
approximately halfway between "good" and "excellent." This
was interpreted as an expression of satisfaction with and
enjoyment of the program.

A comparison of pretest and posttest scores on the
SUPERVISORY INVENTORY ON HUMAN RELATIONS revealed gains
significant at the .02 level or better for nine of the ten
programs. In other words, in all of the programs except
the University Institute of March 16-20, 1953, the gains in
scores from pretest to posttest were sufficiently large to
be attributed to chance less than one time in fifty. The
conclusion can be drawn, then, that the trainees in nine of
the ten programs benefited in increased knowledge as
measured by the Inventory.

As a further measure of program effectiveness an analysis
was made of the responses to each of the one hundred
Inventory items to determine which ones showed significant
changes from pretest to posttest. The purpose of this
analysis was to find out if the majority of the foremen had
learned a few facts and principles or whether there was a
wide variation in the type of changes that were taking
place.

In the ten different programs it was found that the
responses to a total of nine different items changed
significantly (at the .05 level) from pretest to posttest.
One of the items showed significant changes in three
different programs. The direction of change was from

82

"Agree" to "Disagree" and the item read: The person with the highest intelligence, best personality and most experience should always be selected for the job.

The responses to another item showed significant changes in two programs. The change was from "Disagree" to "Agree." The item was as follows: A knowledge of learning curves and plateaus is important to a supervisor.

The other seven items which revealed changes significant at the .05 level follow:

Item No.		Direction of Change
1.	Intelligence consists of what we've learned since we were born.	"A" to "DA"
2.	The well-trained working force is a result of maintaining a large training department.	"DA" to "A"[2]
3.	A good supervisor must be able to do all the jobs performed by the workers he supervises.	"A" to "DA"
4.	A supervisor should accept and carry out any order he receives from an important representative of another department.	"A" to "DA"
5.	Asking the worker to criticise his own work will do more harm than good.	"A" to "DA"

6.   The best way to train a new   "A" to "DA"
      worker is to have him watch
      a good worker at the job.

7.   The training needs of a   "DA" to "A"
      department should be
      determined by the supervisor
      in charge.

[2]This was the only item which showed a significant change from the correct to the incorrect response.

The average gain in score from pretest to posttest for the ten programs was 4.8. Since an average of 1.1 items per program showed significant change in the desired direction, it seems quite clear that there was considerable dispersion of facts and principles which the foremen learned from the sessions. It is apparent that within each program and for all programs combined, different supervisors understood and accepted different facts and principles. Such factors as previous knowledge, job conditions, and effectiveness of the instructors were probably contributing factors.

During the course of evaluating these ten Human Relations Programs, it was decided that several related problems also should be investigated. Consequently, four additional questions were considered in the study.

How Valid Is the SUPERVISORY INVENTORY ON HUMAN RELATIONS As a Measure of Job Performance? In order to determine the validity of the Inventory as a measure of job performance, pretest scores were correlated with the performance rankings of the supervisors in the two private companies involved in this investigation. In the Wisconsin paper mill the relationship was found to be +.35. In the Iowa company a correlation of -.15 was discovered.

From these findings the conclusion can be drawn that in the Wisconsin company the Inventory measured job performance significantly. Those foremen who scored highest on the pretest had a definite tendency to perform best on the job.

In the Iowa company, the Inventory cannot be considered to be a measure of job performance. The negative correlation means that foremen who perform best on the job tended to score lowest on the pretest, but the figure is too small to be significant.

Which Items on the Inventory Can Be Used in the Selection of Supervisors? In the two private companies, the ranked foremen were divided into an upper and lower half. The upper half was considered to be "good" supervisors and the lower half "poor" supervisors. The responses to each of the one hundred items by the "good" foremen were compared with the responses by the "poor" foremen in the companies separately.

In the Wisconsin paper mill, four items discriminated between "good" and "poor" foremen. On all of these items, the "good" foremen tended to have the item correct while the "poor" ones answered it incorrectly. The discriminating items were:

1. A good supervisor must be able to do all the jobs performed by the workers he supervises.
2. The more details a supervisor handles by himself, the better executive he is likely to be.

3. The personnel department or training department should be responsible to see that training is done in all departments.
4. The best way to train a new worker is to have him watch a good worker at the job.

Only one item discriminated between the "good" and "poor" foremen of the Iowa company. The "good" foremen responded correctly to the item which read: A good instruction rule is to emphasize how not to do the job.

If the ranking procedure used in the two companies can be considered to be valid, then four items can be used in the selection of new supervisors in the Wisconsin firm and one item in the Iowa company. This study indicates that those supervisory candidates who answer the items correctly will tend to become good supervisors.

Which Foremen Seem to Benefit Most from the Human Relations Training? The gain in Inventory score from pretest to posttest was used as the measure of benefit derived. The gain was then correlated with age, education, company experience, supervisory experience, number of employees supervised, and on-the-job performance. The correlations were computed for each of the two companies separately.

The only significant relationship was found in the Wisconsin paper mill in which the foremen with the fewest number of employees to supervise benefited most from the program. The correlation was found to be .48. No significant relationships were found between gains and other factors.

What Subject Matter Should Be Stressed in Future University Institutes? The assumption was made that the knowledges and attitudes of the foremen and supervisors who attended the six Institutes involved in this study may be considered to be indicative of the knowledges and attitudes of foremen and supervisors who will attend future similar Institutes. Based on this assumption, the incorrect responses to the pretest by the eighty-four foremen who attended the six University Institutes were tabulated. Those items which should be stressed in future Institutes because they were answered incorrectly by more than half of the foremen were as follows:

1. In training a worker, the first thing the supervisor should do is show in detail how the job is performed.
2. Intelligence consists of what we've learned since we were born.
3. A worker of average intelligence should be able to do a job after he is told and shown how it should be done.
4. The best way to train a new worker is to have him watch a good worker at the job.
5. If we know a worker well, we can always tell what he'll do in a given situation.
6. Anyone is able to do almost any job if he tries hard enough.
7. Attitudes are usually based on a careful study of the facts.
8. If we have an efficient, intelligent, ambitious, and likeable worker in our department, we should do everything we can to keep him there.
9. The well-trained working force is a result of maintaining a large training department.

10. If a supervisor knows all about the work to be done, he is therefore qualified to teach a worker how to do it.
11. Everyone is either an introvert or an extrovert.
12. The best way to overcome frustrations is to fight vigorously.
13. A supervisor should accept and carry out any order he receives from an important representative of another department.

Conclusions

1. The SUPERVISORY INVENTORY ON HUMAN RELATIONS was found to be a reliable instrument for measuring human relations facts and principles. However, its validity as a measure of the job performance of industrial foremen and supervisors must be determined for each company in which it is used.
2. Human relations programs as defined in this study are enjoyed by foremen and supervisors who attend them. These enrollees are well satisfied with both the subject content and the discussion technique used.
3. Knowledges of most foremen and supervisors improve as a result of attendance and participation in human relations programs. This seems to hold true for foremen enrolled in outside-the-plant institutes and conferences as well as those attending in-plant programs in which an outside consultant conducts the sessions.
4. Human relations training programs which are concentrated over a period of five consecutive days seem to be equally effective as those spaced over a period of several weeks or months.

5. A supervisor's age, education, years of company experience, years of supervisory experience, and performance on the job have no significant relationship to the increased knowledges and improved attitudes that result from attendance and participation in the program.

6. Foremen attending human relations programs differ in the subject matter that they learn and accept. Different foremen understand and agree with different facts and principles.

7. Certain items of the SUPERVISORY INVENTORY ON HUMAN RELATIONS can be used in the selection of new supervisors. The specific items that can be used by a particular company should be selected by determining the power of each item to discriminate between "good" and "poor" foremen in that company.

8. A considerable amount of the subject matter discussed in human relations training programs is understood and accepted by a majority of the foremen before the program begins. However, as many as eighty per cent of the foremen disagree with other facts and principles that are going to be discussed.

Recommendations

Recommendations for the Industrial Management Institute of the University of Wisconsin:

1. In order to make the University Institutes and Conferences more effective, the needs of the enrollees should be determined prior to the start of the program. The information included in Exhibit P of this study provides an indication of the knowledges and attitudes that the foremen and supervisors bring

with them to the Institute. Items which were answered incorrectly by most of the foremen can be interpreted as representing their needs.

2. Instruction techniques should be improved in order to increase the number of facts and principles that are understood and accepted by the foremen who attend. This investigation shows that many of the supervisors disagreed with important subject topics at the close of the program. Also, it was found that many of the changes in response from pretest to posttest were made from the correct to the incorrect answer.

3. Institutes, consisting of four and one-half consecutive days, and Conferences, consisting of four spaced one-day meetings, should continue to be offered to meet the expressed needs of the participating companies. Both types of programs were found to be effective in improving knowledges and in changing attitudes.

Recommendations for the Two Private Companies Involved in This Study:

1. In order to make future Company Programs effective, the needs of the enrollees should be determined prior to the start of the program. A tabulation of the incorrect responses to the posttest will reveal the facts and principles that are not understood and accepted by the supervisors. From this information, the basic subject matter for a follow-up program can be determined satisfactorily.

2. A technique should be devised to see whether or not the facts and principles that were learned in the Human Relations Program are being applied on the job. This study reveals that the Company Programs were

effective in increasing knowledge which was the immediate objective of both programs. However, since the long range purpose of the training was to improve performance on the job, efforts should be made to find evidences of better supervisory performance.

3. The study results reveal that some of the supervisors showed no improvement in Inventory scores from pretest to posttest. This suggests that individual counseling interviews should be held with each foreman to discuss those items on the Inventory which he answered incorrectly. From these interviews, the reasons for not accepting the facts and principles that were discussed can usually be ascertained. This information would prove valuable in improving the effectiveness of future programs.

4. A ranking of supervisors from best to poorest on the basis of job performance was made for both companies. This ranking should be used in further research work to determine the validity of tests or other measures to discriminate between good and poor supervisors. Any measures found to be valid can then be used in selecting new supervisors.

5. Four Inventory items were found to discriminate significantly between "good" and "poor" supervisors in the Wisconsin paper mill and one such valid item was discovered for the Iowa manufacturing company. These items should be combined with other measures that discriminate between "good" and "poor" supervisors in order to develop valid procedures for selecting new foremen.

6. Instruction techniques should be studied carefully to determine which ones are most effective in improving attitudes and increasing knowledge. Although the programs were found to be generally effective, this

study shows clearly that many of the facts and principles discussed were not accepted by the foremen.

Recommendations for Further Research:

1. The SUPERVISORY INVENTORY ON HUMAN RELATIONS was found to be a highly reliable instrument. It proved to be a valid Inventory for measuring job performance in only one of the two companies, however. Further comparisons of Inventory scores with job performance should be made to determine whether the test can be used as a valid measure of job performance.

2. Four items on the Inventory discriminated between "good" and "poor" foremen in one plant while only one item discriminated significantly in another plant. Further research is needed in order to build a test of items which discriminate. Such a test could be useful as an instrument for determining the effectiveness of human relations programs as well as a device for selecting new supervisors.

3. In the programs studied in this investigation, a number of instruction techniques were used. Further study should be made to determine which techniques are most effective in teaching human relations facts and principles under varying conditions.

4. A paper-and-pencil Inventory was used as the principal measuring instrument for this study. There also is an urgent need to develop a well controlled technique for evaluating human relations programs by using production criteria or other measures of job performance.

Human relations training programs for industrial foremen and supervisors have been accepted by many companies as the answer to all of the grievance and morale problems in their plants. Because one plant in a community or in a particular type of industry inaugurated such a program, its neighbors and competitors felt that they should have one too. Consequently, the number of companies conducting human relations training for their foremen grew tremendously. Subject matter, instruction techniques, and other details were copied with amazing exactness.

It is hoped that the techniques and finding of this investigation will stimulate the determination of training needs and the objective evaluation of training results by those persons who will be concerned with human relations programs for supervisors from industry and business.

BIBLIOGRAPHY

1. American Society of Training Directors. "Research
        Needed in Industrial Training." Journal of
        Industrial Training. May – June, 1950.

2. Aspley, J.C., and Whitmore, E. The Handbook of
        Industrial Relations. Chicago: Dartnell Press, 1948.

3. Beckman, R. O. How to Train Supervisors. New York:
        Harper & Brothers, 1952.

4. Center, Ralph. "A Human Relations Training Program."
        Journal of Applied Psychology. February, 1951.

5. Chaple, E. D., and Donald, Gordon. "A Method for
        Evaluating Supervisory Personnel." Harvard Business
        Review. Harvard University Graduate School of
        Business Administration, Winter 1946.

6. Cronbach, Lee J. Essentials of Psychological Testing.
        New York: Harper & Brothers, 1949

7. Fern, George. Training for Supervision in Industry. New
        York: McGraw-Hill Book Company, Inc., 1945.

8. File, Q. W. "The Measurement of Supervisory Qualities
        in Industry." Journal of Applied Psychology, 1945.
        29:323 – 337.

9. File, Q. W., and Remmers, H. H., HOW SUPERVISE? New
    York: The Psychological Corporation, 1943.

10. File, Q. W., and Remmers, H. H. Revised Manual, HOW
    SUPERVISE? New York: The Psychological Corporation,
    1948.

11. Fleishman, Edwin A. Leadership Climate and Supervisory
    Behavior. Unpublished Dissertation. Ohio State
    University, 1951.

12. Gardner, Burleigh. Human Relations in Industry.
    Chicago: Richard D. Irwin, Inc., 1945.

13. Good, C. V., Barr, A. S., and Scates, D. E. The
    Methodology of Educational Research. New York:
    D. Appleton – Century Company. 1941.

14. Guilford, J. P. Fundamental Statistics in Psychology
    and Education. New York: McGraw – Hill Book Company,
    Inc., 1942.

15. Habbe, S. "Management Training for Foremen." Conference
    Board Management Record, 1949. 11:16 – 18

16. Hariton, Theodore. Conditions Influencing the Effects
    of Training Foremen in New Human Relations
    Principles. Unpublished Dissertation, University of
    Michigan, 1951.

17. Harvey, O. L. "Measuring the Value of Training."
    Personnel. July, 1946. 23:43 – 45

18. Jennings, Eugene E. A Study of the Relationship of Some Aspects of Personality to Supervisory Success. Unpublished Dissertation, State University of Iowa, 1952.

19. Jennings, Eugene E. Techniques of Successful Foremanship. Wisconsin Commerce Studies, Bureau of Business Research and Service, School of Commerce, University of Wisconsin, 1954.

20. Jennings, Eugene E. Improving Supervisory Behavior. Wisconsin Commerce Studies, Bureau of Business Research and Service, School of Commerce, University of Wisconsin, 1954.

21. Jucius, M. J. Personnel Management. Chicago: Richard D. Irwin, Inc., 1947.

22. Jurgensen, C. E. "Foremen Training Based on the Test: HOW SUPERVISE?" Personnel Journal, 1949. 28:123 – 127.

23. Katz, D. "Morale and Motivation in Industry." Current Trends in Industrial Psychology. University of Pittsburgh Press, 1949.

24. Katzell, Raymond. "Testing a Training Program in Human Relations." Personnel Psychology, 1948. 1:319 – 329.

25. Katzell, Raymond. Can We Evaluate Training? Mimeographed by Industrial Management Institute, University of Wisconsin, April, 1952.

26. Keachie, Edward C. "How Effective is Your Training Program." Journal of Industrial Training. September – October, 1947.

27. Knowles, A. S., and Thompson, R. D. Industrial Management. New York: The MacMillan Company, 1944.

28. Lawshe, C. H. Principles of Personnel Testing. New York: McGraw – Hill Book Company, Inc., 1948.

29. Likert, Rensis. "A Technique for the Measurement of Attitudes." Archives de Psychologie. University of Geneva, 1932. 22:140.

30. Lindbom, Theodore R. Supervisory Training and Employee Attitudes. Unpublished Dissertation, University of Minnesota, 1952.

31. Lindquist, E. F. (ed.) Educational Measurement. Washington: American Council on Education, 1950.

32. Mahler, Walter, and Monroe, Willys. How Industry Determines the Need for and Effectiveness of Training. Personnel Research Section Report 929. New York: The Psychological Corporation, 1952.

33. Maier, N. R. F. "A Human Relations Program for Supervisors." Industrial Labor Relations Review, 1948. 1:443 – 464.

34. Maloney, P. W. "Reading Ease Scores for File's HOW SUPERVISE?" Journal of Applied Psychology, 1952. 36:225 – 227.

35. McGehee, William. "The Research Approach to Training" <u>Personnel Series No. 117</u>. New York: American Management Association, 1948.

36. McNemar, Quinn. <u>Psychological Statistics</u>. New York: John Wiley & Sons, Inc., 1949.

37. Miles, Lester S. <u>Brass Hat or Executive</u>. New York: Funk and Wagnalls Company, 1949.

38. Millard, K. A. "Is HOW SUPERVISE? an Intelligence Test?" <u>Journal of Applied Psychology</u>, 1952. 36:221 – 224.

39. Moore, H. <u>Psychology in Business and Industry</u>. New York: McGraw – Hill Book Company, Inc., 1947.

40. Morrison, James H. "Improving Training Tests." <u>Journal of Industrial Training</u>. March – April, 1953.

41. Osterberg, Wesley. <u>Supervisory Inventory</u>. Mimeographed by the Bureau of Industrial and Applied Psychology, University of Wisconsin, 1947.

42. Osterberg, Wesley, and Lindbom, Theodore. "Evaluating Human Relations Training for Supervisors." <u>Advanced Management</u>. September, 1953.

43. Payne, Stanley L. <u>The Art of Asking Questions</u>. Princeton University Press, 1951.

44. Pigors, Paul, and Meyers, C. A. <u>Personnel Administration</u>. New York: McGraw – Hill Book Company, Inc., 1947.

45. Planty, Earl G. "New Methods for Evaluating Supervisory Training." <u>Personnel</u>, 1945. 21:235 – 241.

46. Planty, E. G., McCord, W. W., and Efferson, C. A. <u>Training Employees and Managers</u>. New York: The Ronald Press Co., 1948.

47. Roethlisberger, F. J. "Training Supervisors in Human Relations." <u>Harvard Business Review</u>. Harvard University Press, September, 1951.

48. Roethlisberger, F. J. and Dickson, W. J. <u>Management and the Worker</u>. Cambridge: Harvard University Press, 1939.

49. Solomon, R. L. "An Extension of the Control Group Design." <u>Psychological Bulletin</u>. 1949. 46:137 – 150.

50. Starch, D. <u>How to Develop Your Executive Ability</u>. New York: Harper & Brothers, 1952.

51. Taylor, Bill N. "Appraising a Supervisory Training Program" <u>Journal of Industrial Training</u>. November – December, 1951.

52. Tiffin, Joseph. <u>Industrial Psychology</u>. New York: Prentice Hall, Inc., 1942.

53. Training Materials Exchange Service. <u>Compilation of the Training Materials Listings Appearing in the 1950 Summary and 1952 Supplement</u>. Mimeographed by the American Society of Training Directors. February, 1954.

54. Weiland, Robert. <u>A New Approach to Supervisory Training</u>. Mimeographed by the Industrial Tape Corporation, New Jersey, 1953.

55. Weitz, Joseph, and Nuckols, Robert. "A Validation Study of HOW SUPERVISE?" <u>Journal of Applied Psychology</u>, 1953. 37:7 – 8.

56. Wert, James, Heidt, Charles O., and Ahmann, J. Stanley. <u>Statistical Methods in Educational and Psychological Research</u>. New York: Appleton – Century – Crofts, Inc., 1954.

57. Wickert, R. R. "Relations Between HOW SUPERVISE?, Intelligence, and Education for a Group of Supervisory Candidates in Industry." <u>Journal of Applied Psychology</u>, 1952. 36:301 – 304.

APPENDIX

102

EXHIBIT A

SUBJECT OUTLINE AND SCHEDULE OF A TYPICAL UNIVERSITY INSTITUTE

Monday

    2:00-4:30 P.M. -- THE SUPERVISOR'S ROLE IN MANAGEMENT

        1. The job of the supervisor.
        2. The tools of supervision.
        3. The relationship of supervisors to others in the
           company.
        4. Simple rules of organization.

Discussion Leader: Donald Kirkpatrick; Industrial
Management Institute; University of Wisconsin; Madison

    6:00 P.M. -- Dinner Meeting, Memorial Union, $2.50 per person.
    7:00-8:30 P.M. -- Film and discussion.

Tuesday

    8:30-11:30 A.M. -- UNDERSTANDING PEOPLE

        1. The need for understanding ourselves and others.
        2. The basis for understanding people.
          a. How people differ in industry.
             (1) Aptitudes and capacities.
             (2) Personality and emotions.
             (3) Interests and motivation.
          b. Why people differ.
             (1) Heredity.
             (2) Environment.
          c. Comparing and measuring these differences.

    12:45-4:00 P.M. -- UNDERSTANDING PEOPLE (Continued)

        3. Understanding human behavior.
          a. Feelings and emotions.
          b. The influence of drives or motivation.
          c. Patterns of behavior.
         4. How the supervisor uses this understanding.

Discussion Leader: Norman Allhiser; Industrial
Management Institute; University of Wisconsin; Madison

Wednesday

8:30-11:30 A.M. -- ATTITUDES OF EMPLOYEES AND MANAGEMENT.

    1. What are attitudes?
    2. What creates them?
    3. Characteristics of attitudes.
    4. Typical attitudes.
    5. How the supervisor builds positive attitudes.

Discussion Leader: Max H. Forster; Training Director; S. C. Johnson & Son, Inc.; Racine.

12:45-4:00 P.M. -- THE SUPERVISOR AS A LEADER

    1. The need for leadership in industry.
    2. The characteristics of a leader.
    3. Developing leadership qualities.
    4. Appraising ourselves as leaders.

Discussion Leader: Edward Grosscup; Plant Manager; Island Steel Container Corporation; Chicago.

Thursday

8:30-11:30 A.M. -- THE SUPERVISOR AS AN INSTRUCTOR.

    1. The need for training in industry.
    2. The foundation of successful training.
       a. The learning process.
       b. The principles of learning.
    3. Applying the principles of learning.
       a. Demonstrations of learning.
       b. Evaluation of the learning demonstrations.

12:45-4:00 P.M.-- THE SUPERVISOR AS AN INSTRUCTOR. (Continued)

    4. Determining departmental training needs.
    5. Planning to meet these needs.
    6. The steps of job training.
       a. Preparation
       b. Presentation.
       c. Application.
       d. Follow-up.

Discussion Leader: John Conway; Training Director; A. O. Smith Corporation; Milwaukee.

Friday

8:30-11:30 A.M. -- A PROBLEM OF EMPLOYEE MOTIVATION.

1. Understanding the people involved.
2. The personal conflicts in the situation.
3. Appraising the facts.
4. Solution of the problem.

(This sessions is developed around a recorded case study.)

Discussion Leader: Frank Walsh; Bureau of Personnel; State of Wisconsin; Madison.

12:30-3:00 P.M. -- SUMMARY AND PROBLEM SESSION.

1. Exchanging experiences on typical supervisory problems.
2. Applying the principles discussed to specific problems.
3. Summary

Discussion Leader: M. D. Doyle; Industrial Management Institute, University of Wisconsin; Madison.

3:00-3:30 P.M. -- Comment Sheets and Issuance of Certificates.

EXHIBIT B

WHAT DO WORKERS WANT MOST FROM THEIR JOBS?

Let us try to put ourselves in the worker's shoes and figure out which things he wants most from his job.

Of the following 10 items (all of which are important to him), list in the column "MY RATING" the items in order of importance. Place a "1" after the item you think workers want most, a "2" after the next most important item, etc.

Remember, it's not what you want but what you think the worker wants.

	My Rating	W	F	This Group
1. Help on personal problems				
2. Interesting work				
3. High wages				
4. Job Security				
5. Personal loyalty of foreman				
6. Tactful disciplining				
7. Full appreciation for work done				
8. Feeling of belonging				
9. Good working conditions				
10. Promotion in the company				

EXHIBIT C

FILMS SHOWN AT UNIVERSITY INSTITUTES[1]

There were three films which were shown at all of the six Institutes involved in the investigation. These were:

1. The Inner Man Steps Out
2. Of Pups and Puzzles
3. Instructing the Worker on the Job

In addition, other films were used at the discretion of the discussion leaders. This list of films includes the following:

1. By Jupiter
2. It's Our Job
3. Chuck Hanson, One Guy
4. The Supervisor as a Leader
5. Heredity and Prenatal Care
6. The Boss Didn't Say Good Morning

[1]All films were obtained from the Bureau of Audio-Visual Instruction of the University of Wisconsin Extension Division, Madison.

EXHIBIT D

SUBJECT OUTLINE OF PRIVATE COMPANY
HUMAN RELATIONS PROGRAMS

1. The Duties and Responsibilities of a Supervisor

    Job duties
    Job responsibilities:
        To the company
        To the employees

2. The Principles of Organization
        Why an organization?
        How an organization is built up
        Using an organization effectively -- interdepartmental
            dependency and cooperation
        Simple rules of organization

3. Communications in a Business Organization
        The need for effective communications
        Techniques of communications
        Three-way communications

4. Understanding Human Behavior
        The importance of "people"
        Individual differences in business and industry
        Measuring and evaluating individual differences

5. Understanding Human Behavior (continued)
        Motivation of people
        Motivation and frustration
        Using an understanding of people

6. The Selection of Employees
        The place of job specifications
        Selection techniques
            Interviews
            Historical data
            Tests
        The supervisor's part in selection

7. Orientation and Induction of Employees
        The need for adequate induction and orientation
        Elements of induction
        An induction program that is effective
        The supervisor's part in induction and orientation

8. Training and Developing Employees
   Understanding the learning process
   Principles of learning
   Training techniques

9. Training and Developing Employees (Continued)
   Training employees
         Job training
         Attitude training
         Safety training
   Development of employees

10. Employee-Supervisor Relations
    Order-giving
    Reprimands
    Discipline
    Personal problems
    Grievances

11. Practice Supervision
    Defining the problem
    Getting and analyzing the facts
    Choosing a solution
    Analyzing the principles of supervision involved in
          the case
    (This session to be devoted to a recorded case study.)

12. Leadership
    The need for leadership
    The characteristics of a leader
    Developing leadership qualities
    The supervisor as a leader

EXHIBIT E

COMPANIES SENDING THE MOST FOREMEN TO THE
SIX UNIVERSITY INSTITUTES FROM JANUARY TO JUNE, 1953

Company	City	No. of Foremen
Pabst Brewing Co.	Milwaukee	19
Allen-Bradley Co.	Milwaukee	12
Schlitz Brewing Co.	Milwaukee	11
United States Rubber Co.	Eau Claire	8
Rockford Machine Tool Co.	Rockford, Ill.	7

EXHIBIT F

ITEMS ADOPTED FROM OTHER INVENTORIES FOR INCLUSION IN THE
"SUPERVISORY INVENTORY ON HUMAN RELATIONS"

I. HOW SUPERVISE?(9)

1. Family and financial troubles frequently decrease both the quantity and quality of a worker's output.

2. A good supervisor can tell what a worker is worth the first time he talks with him.

3. The attitude of an employee has very little effect on his production.

4. The worker's opinion of his supervisor is not very important.

5. Keeping the worker afraid of losing his job is the best way to insure that he will do an honest day's work.

6. A good supervisor must be able to do all the jobs performed by the workers he supervises.

7. A supervisor should never admit it to the workers when he makes a wrong decision.

8. The average worker cares little about what others think of his job so long as the pay is good.

9. How a worker thinks he is being treated is usually more important than the treatment he actually receives.

10. Asking the worker to criticize his own work will do more harm than good.

11. The first duty of the supervisor when handling complaints is to show the worker where he is wrong.

12. The best way to handle tough workers is to be tougher than they are.

13. Most employees will do better work when constantly watched by their supervisors.

II. SUPERVISORY INVENTORY (41)

1. Anyone is able to do almost any job if he tries hard enough.

2. An employee will probably get along faster and better if he has two supervisors than if he has only one.

3. Even though an employee is very intelligent and capable, if he is dissatisfied with a job at a low level, he probably will also be dissatisfied with any job at a higher level.

4. A foreman should not praise members of his department when they do a good job, because they will ask for a raise.

5. Grievances and morale problems should be handled by a special department set up for the purpose, rather than by department supervisors.

6. People will work faster and longer if they always have a little more work ahead of them than they can possibly do.

7. When correcting the work an employee has been doing wrong, the foreman should have the other employees observe, so that they won't make the same mistake.

8. An employer has a right to expect that his employees will leave their problems at home.

9. A foreman who notices that one of his men gets nervous and confused whenever he is watched should spend considerable time near him until the nervousness disappears.

III. SELF-ANALYSIS QUIZ FOR SUPERVISORS AND EXECUTIVES (37)

1. If a supervisor knows all about the work to be done, he is therefore qualified to teach a worker how to do it.

2. Lack of interest in their work accounts for more loafing on the part of workers than does mere laziness.

3. A worker's ability to do a given piece of work is always a sure sign that he is satisfied and properly placed.

4. A supervisor cannot be expected to train his workers. He is too busy running his job.

5. <u>Final</u> <u>responsibility</u> of the supervisor for the work of his unit cannot be delegated to anyone else.

6. When reprimanding a worker, it is best to try to humiliate him in order to make the reprimand stick.

7. The more details a supervisor handles by himself, the better executive he is likely to be.

8. The best thing a supervisor can do if he has a trouble-maker in his department is immediately to recommend a dismissal for the worker.

9. A supervisor should accept and carry out any order he receives from an important representative of another department.

10. As long as he gets the work done, a supervisor does not have to set a good example to his men by his personal conduct.

11. The supervisor doing the best job is the one who is always in the shop, loudly pointing out mistakes and spurring the workers on to greater production.

IV. WHAT'S YOUR MANAGEMENT I.Q.? (37)

1. Teaching is complete only when the learner has learned.

2. The motivating factor among most employees is to be paid at the end of the week and to be told what to do.

3. The well-trained working force is a result of maintaining a large training department.

4. The supervisor must be aware of the fundamentals of learning and teaching.

5. In training a worker, the first thing the supervisor should do is show in detail how the job is performed.

6. A good instruction rule is to emphasize how <u>not</u> to do the job.

7. A study of the actions of recognized leaders may greatly increase one's knowledge of leadership.

EXHIBIT G

SUPERVISORY INVENTORY ON HUMAN RELATIONS

Donald L. Kirkpatrick

Following are 100 items concerned with your job as a supervisor.
Some of them deal with background facts while others are statements about your everyday supervisory practices.

Please indicate after each statement whether you agree (A) or
disagree (DA) as follows:

If you agree, circle the "A" thus: DA
If you disagree, circle the "DA" thus: A

PLEASE ANSWER ALL STATEMENTS EVEN IF YOU AREN'T SURE.

Individual Information

Name _____ Title _____
(please print)

Company _____

How Long have you been a Foreman or Supervisor? _____

Have you ever attended classes on Human Relations? Yes___ No ___

Where? _____

Please circle the last year completed.

Grade School   High School   College

3 4 5 6 7 8   1 2 3 4   1 2 3 4 5 6 7

114

These statements concern facts with which a supervisor should be familiar. You probably won't know the correct answers to some of the questions, but please guess.

Correct Responses Are in Bold and Underlined

1. Anyone is able to do almost any job if he tries hard enough. A **DA**

2. People are basically the same and should be treated pretty much alike. A **DA**

3. We are born with certain aptitudes, capacities, and potentials and these tend to limit the things we can do. **A** DA

4. The only kind of recognition that means anything to a worker is more money. A **DA**

5. There is little that a person can do to develop himself as a leader. A **DA**

6. Family and financial troubles frequently decrease both the quantity and quality of a worker's output. **A** DA

7. Intelligence consists of what we've learned since we were kids. A **DA**

8. If we know what kind of a man the father was, we can be almost certain of what kind of a boy his son is. A **DA**

9. Most workers are interested in doing work of which they can be proud. **A** DA

10. If a supervisor knows all about the work to be done, he is therefore qualified to teach a worker how to do it. A **DA**

11. A good supervisor can tell what a worker is worth the first time he talks with him. A **DA**

12. Everyone is either an introvert or an extrovert. A **DA**

13. Heredity refers to everything that has happened to us since we were born. A **DA**

14. Frustration means that something is blocking the wishes or desires of an individual. **A** DA

15. Teaching is complete only when the learner has learned. **A** DA

16. Lack of interest in their work accounts for more loafing on the part of workers than does mere laziness. **A** DA

17. Introverts and extroverts should be put on a job where they work together, because they can get along very well. A **DA**

18. If we know a worker well, we can always tell what he'll do in a given situation. A **DA**

19. We are born with certain attitudes and there is little we can do to change them. A **DA**

20. Attitudes are usually based on a careful study of the facts. A **DA**

21. A worker's ability to do a given piece of work is always a sure sign that he is satisfied and properly placed. A **DA**

22. An introvert likes to work with others and is usually the "life of the party".   A **DA**

23. Workers are faced with frustrating situations almost every day.   **A** DA

24. The older we are, the more fixed are our attitudes.   **A** DA

25. The best way to overcome frustrations is to fight vigorously.   A **DA**

26. The motivating factor among most employees is to be paid at the end of the week and to be told what to do.   A **DA**

27. The attitude of an employee has very little effect on his production.   A **DA**

28. The person with the highest intelligence, best person- ality and most experience should always be selected for a job.   A **DA**

PART II   KNOW-HOW

These statements are concerned with principles of supervision. Some questions will be easy to answer, while others will be difficult.

29. An employee will probably get along faster and better if he has two supervisors than if he has only one.   A **DA**

30. Even though an employee is very intelligent and capable, if he is dissatisfied with a job at a low level, he probably will also be dissatisfied with any job at a higher level.   A **DA**

31. The worker's opinion of his supervisor is not very important.   A **DA**

32. A foreman should not praise members of his department when they do a good job, because they will ask for a raise.   A **DA**

33. A supervisor cannot be expected to train his workers. He is too busy running his job.   A **DA**

34. A supervisor should be able to solve his own problems without getting all the detailed facts.   A **DA**

35. Grievances and morale problems should be handled by a special department set up for the purpose, rather than by department supervisors.   A **DA**

36. People will work faster and longer if they always have a little more work ahead of them than they can possibly do.   A **DA**

37. Keeping the worker afraid of losing his job is the best way to insure that he will do an honest day's work.   A **DA**

38. When correcting the work an employee has been doing wrong, the foreman should have the other employees observe, so that they won't make the same mistake.   A **DA**

116

39. The well-trained working force is a result of maintaining a large training department. **A** **DA**

40. A group of people can usually find a better solution to a problem than one individual. **A** DA

41. A good supervisor must be able to do all the jobs performed by the workers he supervises. A **DA**

42. An employer has a right to expect that his employees will leave their problems at home. A **DA**

43. A supervisor should never admit it to the workers when he makes a wrong decision. A **DA**

44. A knowledge of personalities involved helps in solving a problem. **A** DA

45. Final responsibility of the supervisor for the work of his unit cannot be delegated to anyone else. **A** DA

46. A foreman who notices that one of his men gets nervous and confused whenever he is watched should spend considerable time near him until the nervousness disappears. A **DA**

47. When reprimanding a worker, it is best to try to humiliate him in order to make the reprimand stick. A **DA**

48. A supervisor can't be bothered to give the worker reasons for changes which he is asked to make in his work. A **DA**

49. The supervisor must be aware of the fundamentals of learning and teaching. **A** DA

50. A supervisor would get himself into trouble or else lose respect if he asked workers to help him solve problems that concern them. A **DA**

51. The more details a supervisor handles by himself, the better executive he is likely to be. A **DA**

52. The average worker cares little about what others think of his job so long as the pay is good. A **DA**

53. The best thing a supervisor can do if he has a trouble-maker in his department is immediately to recommend a dismissal for the worker. A **DA**

54. In training a worker, the first thing the supervisor should do is show in detail how the job is performed. A **DA**

55. It's a bad policy for a supervisor to tell a worker, "I don't know the answer to your question, but I'll find out and let you know. A **DA**

56. A supervisor should accept and carry out any order he receives from an important representative of another department. A **DA**

57. How a worker thinks he is being treated is usually more important than the treatment he actually receives. **A** DA

58. Asking the worker to criticise his own work will do more harm than good.   A **DA**

59. A good instruction rule is to emphasize how <u>not</u> to do the job.   A **DA**

60. Most bosses fail because they don't have the technical know-how for the job.   A **DA**

61. It is important to understand ourselves before we can understand others.   **A** DA

62. Attitudes of employees are greatly influenced by the attitudes of their supervisor.   **A** DA

63. The first duty of the supervisor when handling complaints is to show the worker where he is wrong.   A **DA**

64. The personnel department or training department should be responsible to see that training is done in all departments.   A **DA**

65. It is best not to give a raise unless a worker asks for it.   A **DA**

66. I have more problems in my company than the average supervisor in other companies.   A **DA**

67. A supervisor should be an introvert; otherwise he would spend all day talking with others in the plant and would accomplish very little.   A **DA**

68. Most workers have a bad attitude toward the company because they don't feel they get paid enough.   A **DA**

69. The best way to handle tough workers is to be tougher than they are.   A **DA**

70. A worker of average intelligence should be able to do a job after he is told and shown how it should be done.   A **DA**

71. If we have an efficient, intelligent, ambitious, and likeable worker in our department, we should do everything we can to keep him there.   A **DA**

72. The supervisor is closer to his workers than he is to management.   **A** DA

73. A supervisor would be wasting his time by spending a lot of time talking with his employees about their families, interests, and outside-the-plant problems.   A **DA**

74. Most employees will do better work when constantly watched by their supervisor.   A **DA**

75. A knowledge of learning curves and plateaus is important to a supervisor.   **A** DA

76. If we have problems bothering us, we should keep them to ourselves and solve them the best way we can.   A **DA**

77. A supervisor should represent the workers to top management.   **A** DA

118

78. Most workers would like to feel that they can go to their foremen for help, sympathy, or advise. **A** DA

79. Workers who have bad attitudes should be ignored and encouraged to quit. A **DA**

80. As long as he gets the work done, a supervisor does not have to set a good example to his men by his personal conduct. A **DA**

81. It is a good idea to tell a worker he has done a good job in front of other workers. **A** DA

82. The best way to train a new worker is to have him watch a good worker at the job. A **DA**

83. Follow-up to see how a worker is doing isn't necessary if he got started in the right way. A **DA**

84. Even if he thinks it is wrong a supervisor should do whatever his boss tells him to do without questioning it. A **DA**

85. Criticizing a worker for his mistakes will bring better results than praising him for his good work. A **DA**

86. The supervisor doing the best job is the one who is always in the shop, loudly pointing out mistakes and spurring the workers on to greater productions. A **DA**

87. Before deciding on the solution to a problem, a list of possible solutions should be made and compared. **A** DA

88. A supervisor should keep his boss informed of what's going on. **A** DA

89. A better understanding of people will result in higher morale and more production. **A** DA

90. A study of the actions of recognized leaders may greatly increase one's knowledge of leadership. **A** DA

91. A supervisor should be willing to listen to almost everything the workers want to tell him. **A** DA

92. A supervisor should have someone trained to take over his job. **A** DA

93. The worker should look toward the steward and the union for leadership rather than toward the supervisor. A **DA**

94. The supervisor can do very little to make his workers happy because company policy controls such things as wages, vacations and bonuses. A **DA**

95. A supervisor should always display a friendly manner towards his workers. **A** DA

96. The training needs of a department should be determined by the supervisor in charge. **A** DA

97. A supervisor in a large department should never delegate any of his authority to a subordinate; he should delegate only responsibility. A **DA**

119

98. A supervisor doesn't have to be a leader if he has all the technical know-how for the job.   A **DA**

99. It pays for the supervisor to spend a lot of time with a new employee to be sure he is well trained on his first job.   **A** DA

100. Courses on Human Relations are of very little value. We should be learning more about the technical aspects of our job.   A **DA**

EXHIBIT H

USE OF PEARSON PRODUCT-MOMENT AND SPEARMAN-BROWN FORMULAS (14)

The Pearson Product-Moment formula can be used to determine the relationship between two factors. The coefficient of correlation (r) is an expression of that relationship. The higher the r, the closer the relationship. The Pearson formula for calculating r may be written as follows:

$$r = \frac{N(\Sigma\ XY) - \Sigma\ X\Sigma\ Y}{\sqrt{N\Sigma\ X^2 - (\Sigma\ X)^2}\sqrt{N\Sigma\ Y^2 - (\Sigma\ Y)^2}}$$

In this formula:
  r = coefficient of correlation
  N = number of cases
  Σ = summation
  X = one factor
  Y = other factor

The reliability of a test can be determined by using this formula. By dividing the test in half on the basis of odd and even items, the reliability coefficients of correlation can be computed.

An example (40:26) illustrating the computation of r follows:

PEARSON COEFFICIENT OF CORRELATION

Students (N)	Score on odd items (X)	Score on even items (Y)	X^2	Y^2	XY
A	20	29	400	841	580
B	23	24	529	576	552
C	29	25	841	625	725
D	31	38	961	1,444	1,178
E	33	28	1,089	784	924
F	38	40	1,444	1,600	1,520
G	39	34	1,521	1,156	1,326
H	40	34	1,600	1,156	1,360
I	43	40	1,849	1,600	1,720
J	44	48	1,936	2,304	2,112
	340	340	12,170	12,086	11,997

$$r = \frac{10(11,977) - 340(340)}{\sqrt{10(12,170) - (340)^2}\ \sqrt{10(12,086) - (340)^2}}$$

$$r = \frac{4,370}{\sqrt{6100}\sqrt{5260}} = \frac{4,370}{5,662.3}$$

$$r = 77.2 \quad [1]$$

[1] Editor's Note: Original investigator added a handwritten answer for r of .772 at a later, unknown date.

The correlation coefficient just derived is for one-half of the test only. In order to estimate the reliability of the whole test, the Spearman-Brown formula is used:

$$r_t = \frac{2r}{1 + r}$$

where r_t is the reliability coefficient of the whole test and r is the coefficient of correlation calculated by the Pearson formula. In the example used above, the computation would be as follows:

$$r_t = \frac{2(77.2)}{1 + 77.2}$$

$$r_t = .871$$

EXHIBIT I

I N D U S T R I A L   M A N A G E M E N T   I N S T I T U T E
C O M M E N T   S H E E T

I. <u>DISCUSSION LEADERS</u>

                                                                E G F P

1. NAME _____   ☐ ☐ ☐ ☐

(Reasons) _____

_____

                                                                E G F P

2. NAME _____   ☐ ☐ ☐ ☐

(Reasons) _____

_____

                                                                  E G F P

3. NAME _____   ☐ ☐ ☐ ☐

(Reasons) _____

_____

                                                                  E G F P

4. NAME _____   ☐ ☐ ☐ ☐

(Reasons) _____

_____

                                                                  E G F P

5. NAME _____   ☐ ☐ ☐ ☐

(Reasons) _____

_____

                                                                  E G F P

6. NAME _____   ☐ ☐ ☐ ☐

(Reasons) _____

_____

                                                                  E G F P

7. NAME _____   ☐ ☐ ☐ ☐

(Reasons) _____

_____

                                                                  E G F P

8. NAME _____   ☐ ☐ ☐ ☐

(Reasons) _____

_____

(over)

124

II. I suggest the following people for future discussion leaders:

NAME   COMPANY   SUBJECT

_____

_____

III. I found the following subjects most useful and/or interesting:

_____

_____

_____

IV. I found the following subjects least useful and/or interesting:

_____

_____

_____

V. The following subjects should be considered on future programs:

_____

_____

_____

VI. Use this space for recommendations, suggestions, or other comments
      about the program.

_____

_____

_____

_____

_____

_____

EXHIBIT J

COMPUTATION OF "T" SCORES (36:221)

In order to compute the "t" score, the mean gain (Mg) and the standard deviation (S.D.) of the Mg were first computed. (See any basic statistics book for this computation.) The next step was the calculation of the estimated standard error of the mean (Sm) by the following formula.

$$Sm = \frac{S.D.}{\sqrt{N-1}}$$

in which N = the number of individuals being measured.

"T" was then computed by the formula:

$$t = \frac{Mg}{Sm}$$

For an example, the figures from the University Institute of January 12 – 16, 1953 will be used.

N = 22   Mg = 5.0   S.D. = 3.3

Then:

$$Sm = \frac{3.3}{\sqrt{22-1}} = \frac{3.3}{4.6} = .72$$

$$t = \frac{5.0}{.72} = 6.9$$

Reference to a "t" table (36:368) revealed that for an N of 22, this t of 6.9 corresponds to a P (probability) of less than .001. This means that less than one time in a thousand will a mean gain as large as 5.0 occur as a result of chance. It can be stated with near certainty, then, that this Institute was effective according to the gains from pretest to posttest.

EXHIBIT K

SUPERVISORY MERIT RATING FORM -- IOWA MANUFACTURING COMPANY

The form for periodically rating the performance of the
supervisors in this Iowa company contained ten factors. These
factors include: quality of work, application to work, attitude
and cooperation, ability to handle people, adaptability and
ability to accept responsibility, safety and housekeeping,
dependability, judgment, responsibility of job, and knowledge of
job.

Each of these ten factors was weighted equally. A
supervisor could receive a point value of 30 on each factor or a
total of 300 points on the rating form.

As an example, the description and break down of one of the
factors is as follows:

Judgment – Are his decisions wise? Are his decisions
logical in the absence of detailed instructions on such matters
as safety, quality, limits, etc.? Has he proven himself in
emergency decisions?

1 2 3 4 5	6 7 8 9 10	11 12 13 14 15
Poor – Usually mistaken.	Fair – Ability to handle unusual situations doubtful	Normal – Some errors, but usually shows avg. judgment.

16 17 18 19 20	21 22 23 24 25	26 27 28 29 30
Above Normal – Usually logical. Few errors in judgment	Good – Nearly always logical decisions. Handles emergencies well.	Excellent – Thinks quickly and logically. Judgments outstanding.

The rater proceeds to circle the number best describing the
performance of the supervisor. The circled numbers for each of
the ten factors are added together to determine the total points
for the supervisor.

Since four raters fill out the form for each supervisor, the four point totals are added together and divided by four to compute the final rating score for each foreman.

EXHIBIT L

SUPERVISORY RANKING FORM -- WISCONSIN PAPER MILL

Please rank these supervisors and foremen in order of their
overall performance on the job. Keep in mind their:
   1. Administrative skills -- planning, organizing,
      coordinating.
   2. Ability to handle and get along with their subordinates.
   3. Knowledge of the work under their supervision.

Alphabetical Order   Rank Order*
                                  (from best to poorest)
   1.   1.

   2.   2.

   3.   3.

   4.   4.

   5.   5.

   6.   6.

   7.   7.

   8.   8.

   9.   9.

                  Signed _____

*Perhaps the easiest way to rank them is to start at the extreme --
pick out the best one, then the poorest, then the second best, etc.

EXHIBIT M

CONVERSION OF RANK ORDER OF SUPERVISORS
TO A FIVE POINT SCALE (28)

In order to combine the rankings of the four management persons who rated the supervisors, it was necessary to convert the rank order into a five point scale. The four columns below illustrate how this was accomplished.

Rank Order (1)	Point Value (2)	Rank Order (3)	Point Value (4)
1	5	1	5
2	4	2	4
3	3	3	4
4	3	4	3
5	3	5	3
6	2	6	3
7	1	7	2
		8	2
		9	1

If a supervisor, for example, was ranked by one of the raters as the second best supervisor of the group of seven (column 1), he would be assigned a point value of 4 (column 2). If another ranker had placed him in fifth best out of the seven (column 1), he would receive 3 additional points (column 2). The total points were then accumulated from the four independent rankings.

In the case where nine foremen were ranked, column 3 and 4 were used.

EXHIBIT N

USE OF RANK-DIFFERENCE CORRELATION (36:97)

A simple way of calculating the relationship between two factors is the use of the rank-difference method of correlation. The individuals are ranked in order for each of the two factors. In a tie, the ranks are split between the individuals who are tied. If two individuals shared third and fourth places, each would be assigned a rank of 3.5. If three individuals were tied for third, each would be assigned a rank of 4 since they shared third, fourth, and fifth places.

An example of the calculation of rho, the rank difference measure of correlation follows:

CALCULATION OF RANK-DIFFERENCE CORRELATION

Scores		Ranks		Differences	
1st Trial	2nd Trial	1st	2nd	d	d^2
88	40	3	1.0	2.0	4.00
95	46	4	2.0	2.0	4.00
202	135	10	10.0	0.0	0.00
176	98	8	4.5	3.5	12.25
118	115	5	6.0	1.0	1.00
186	137	9	11.0	2.0	4.00
74	63	1	3.0	2.0	4.00
78	117	2	7.0	5.0	25.00
306	294	13	13.0	0.0	0.00
211	98	11	4.5	6.5	42.25
158	132	7	8.5	1.5	2.25
151	132	6	8.5	2.5	6.25
230	237	12	12.0	0.0	0.00

$$105.00 = \Sigma d^2$$

$$\text{rho} = 1 - \frac{6\Sigma d^2}{N(N^2 - 1)}$$

$$\text{rho} = 1 - \frac{6(105)}{13(169 - 1)} = 1 - \frac{630}{2184} = .71$$

EXHIBIT O

CALCULATION OF CHI SQUARE BY MEANS

OF A FOURFOLD CONTIGENCY TABLE (36:200)

In order to determine whether or not dichotomous items on the Inventory discriminated between "good" and "poor" foremen, chi square was computed. This chi square formula makes use of a fourfold contingency table which can be set up as follows:

A	B	A + B
C	D	C + D

A+C   B+D

Chi square can then be computed from:

$$x^2 = \frac{N(AD - BC)^2}{(A + B)\,(C + D)\,(A + C)\,(B + D)}$$

Reference to a chi square table will indicate the probability of chance alone having caused the difference between the responses of "good" and "poor" foremen.

For an example, the data accumulated for item number 82 of the SUPERVISORY INVENTORY ON HUMAN RELATIONS will be used. The tabulation was made for the foremen in the Wisconsin paper mill involved in this study.

It was found that 8 of the "good" foremen had the item wrong while 6 had it right. Of the "poor" foremen, all 15 had the item wrong. Hence, the fourfold contingency table would be as follows:

Item 82

	right	wrong	
good	6	8	14
poor	0	15	15
	6	23	29

The data were then inserted in the chi square formula thus:

$$x^2 = \frac{29(90 - 0)^2}{(14)\,(15)\,(6)\,(23)} = 8.1$$

Reference to a chi square table (36:367) reveals that the probability is .01. This means that less than one time in a hundred would the difference between the way "good" and "poor" foremen answered the item result from chance alone. Therefore, it can be stated with near certainty that this item discriminated between the "good" and "poor" foremen of the Wisconsin paper mill.

EXHIBIT P

PERCENT OF INCORRECT RESPONSES ON PRETEST BY EIGHTY-FOUR FOREMEN
ATTENDING UNIVERSITY INSTITUTES BETWEEN JANUARY AND JUNE, 1953

PART I   KNOW-WHAT

These statements concern facts with which a supervisor should be familiar. You probably won't know the correct answers to some of the questions, but please guess.

		% Incorrect			% Incorrect
		A DA			A DA
1.	Anyone is able to do almost any job if he tries hard enough.	**63**	12.	Everyone is either an introvert or an extrovert.	**51**
2.	People are basically the same and should be treated pretty much alike.	**33**	13.	Heredity refers to everything that has happened to us since we were born.	**6**
3.	We are born with certain aptitudes, capacities, and potentials and these tend to limit the things we can do.	**33**	14.	Frustration means that something is blocking the wishes or desires of an individual.	**15**
4.	The only kind of recognition that means anything to a worker is more money.	**9**	15.	Teaching is complete only when the learner has learned.	**23**
5.	There is little that a person can do to develop himself as a leader.	**2**	16.	Lack of interest in their work accounts for more loafing on the part of workers than does mere laziness.	**9**
6.	Family and financial troubles frequently decrease both the quantity and quality of a worker's output.	**3**	17.	Introverts and extroverts should be put on a job where they work together, because they can get along very well.	**18**
7.	Intelligence consists of what we've learned since we were kids.	**77**			
8.	If we know what kind of a man the father was, we can be almost certain of what kind of a boy his son is.	**3**	18.	If we know a worker well, we can always tell what he'll do in a given situation.	**68**
9.	Most workers are interested in doing work of which they can be proud.	**7**	19.	We are born with certain attitudes and there is little we can do to change them.	**1**
10.	If a supervisor knows all about the work to be done, he is therefore qualified to teach a worker how to do it.	**51**	20.	Attitudes are usually based on a careful study of the facts.	**58**
11.	A good supervisor can tell what a worker is worth the first time he talks with him.	**3**	21.	A worker's ability to do a given piece of work is always a sure sign that he is satisfied and properly placed.	**43**

22. An introvert likes to work with others and is usually the "life of the party".   A DA   **29**

23. Workers are faced with frustrating situations almost every day.   A DA   **39**

24. The older we are, the more fixed are our attitudes.   A DA   **16**

25. The best way to overcome frustrations is to fight vigorously.   A DA   **51**

26. The motivating factor among most employees is to be paid at the end of the week and to be told what to do.   A DA   **40**

27. The attitude of an employee has very little effect on his production.   A DA   **9**

28. The person with the highest intelligence, best personality and most experience should always be selected for a job.   A DA   **45**

PART II   KNOW-HOW

These statements are concerned with principles of supervision. Some questions will be easy to answer, while others will be difficult.

	% *Incorrect*		*%* *Incorrect*

29. An employee will probably get along faster and better if he has two supervisors than if he has only one.   A DA   **8**

30. Even though an employee is very intelligent and capable, if he is dissatisfied with a job at a low level, he probably will also be dissatisfied with any job at a higher level.   A DA   **15**

31. The worker's opinion of his supervisor is not very important.   A DA   **6**

32. A foreman should not praise members of his department when they do a good job, because they will ask for a raise.   A DA   **3**

33. A supervisor cannot be expected to train his workers. He is too busy running his job.   A DA   **7**

34. A supervisor should be able to solve his own problems without getting all the detailed facts.   A DA   **13**

35. Grievances and morale problems should be handled by a special department set up for the purpose, rather than by department supervisors.   A DA   **29**

36. People will work faster and longer if they always have a little more work ahead of them than they can possibly do.   A DA   **40**

37. Keeping the worker afraid of losing his job is the best way to insure that he will do an honest day's work.   A DA   **5**

38. When correcting the work an employee has been doing wrong, the foreman should have the other employees observe, so that they won't make the same mistake.   A DA   **14**

136

39. The well-trained working force is a result of maintaining a large training department.
A DA
54

40. A group of people can usually find a better solution to a problem than one individual.
A DA
7

41. A good supervisor must be able to do all the jobs performed by the workers he supervises.
A DA
49

42. An employer has a right to expect that his employees will leave their problems at home.
A DA
26

43. A supervisor should never admit it to the workers when he makes a wrong decision.
A DA
5

44. A knowledge of personalities involved helps in solving a problem.
A DA
4

45. Final responsibility of the supervisor for the work of his unit cannot be delegated to anyone else.
A DA
24

46. A foreman who notices that one of his men gets nervous and confused whenever he is watched should spend considerable time near him until the nervousness disappears.
A DA
25

47. When reprimanding a worker, it is best to try to humiliate him in order to make the reprimand stick.
A DA
4

48. A supervisor can't be bothered to give the worker reasons for changes which he is asked to make in his work.
A DA
2

49. The supervisor must be aware of the fundamentals of learning and teaching.
A DA
1

50. A supervisor would get himself into trouble or else lose respect if he asked workers to help him solve problems that concern them.
A DA
2

51. The more details a supervisor handles by himself, the better executive he is likely to be.
A DA
30

52. The average worker cares little about what others think of his job so long as the pay is good.
A DA
21

53. The best thing a supervisor can do if he has a trouble-maker in his department is immediately to recommend a dismissal for the worker.
A DA
7

54. In training a worker, the first thing the supervisor should do is show in detail how the job is performed.
A DA
80

55. It's a bad policy for a supervisor to tell a worker, "I don't know the answer to your question, but I'll find out and let you know.
A DA
16

56. A supervisor should accept and carry out any order he receives from an important representative of another department.
A DA
51

57. How a worker thinks he is being treated is usually more important than the treatment he actually receives.
A DA
23

58. Asking the worker to criticise his own work will do more harm than good.   A DA   **30**

59. A good instruction rule is to emphasize how <u>not</u> to do the job.   A DA   **33**

60. Most bosses fail because they don't have the technical know-how for the job.   A DA   **37**

61. It is important to understand ourselves before we can understand others.   A DA   **5**

62. Attitudes of employees are greatly influenced by the attitudes of their supervisor.   A DA   **5**

63. The first duty of the supervisor when handling complaints is to show the worker where he is wrong.   A DA   **33**

64. The personnel department or training department should be responsible to see that training is done in all departments.   A DA   **43**

65. It is best not to give a raise unless a worker asks for it.   A DA   **2**

66. I have more problems in my company than the average supervisor in other companies.   A DA   **5**

67. A supervisor should be an introvert; otherwise he would spend all day talking with others in the plant and would accomplish very little.   A DA   **19**

68. Most workers have a bad attitude toward the company because they don't feel they get paid enough.   A DA   **17**

69. The best way to handle tough workers is to be tougher than they are.   A DA   **11**

70. A worker of average intelligence should be able to do a job after he is told and shown how it should be done.   A DA   **70**

71. If we have an efficient, intelligent, ambitious, and likeable worker in our department, we should do everything we can to keep him there.   A DA   **58**

72. The supervisor is closer to his workers than he is to management.   A DA   **26**

73. A supervisor would be wasting his time by spending a lot of time talking with his employees about their families, interests, and outside-the-plant problems.   A DA   **8**

74. Most employees will do better work when constantly watched by their supervisor.   A DA   **7**

75. A knowledge of learning curves and plateaus is important to a supervisor.   A DA   **37**

76. If we have problems bothering us, we should keep them to ourselves and solve them the best way we can.   A DA   **5**

77. A supervisor should represent the workers to top management.   A DA   **24**

138

78. Most workers would like to feel that they can go to their foremen for help, sympathy, or advise. A DA **2**

79. Workers who have bad attitudes should be ignored and encouraged to quit. A DA **2**

80. As long as he gets the work done, a supervisor does not have to set a good example to his men by his personal conduct. A DA **6**

81. It is a good idea to tell a worker he has done a good job in front of other workers. A DA **29**

82. The best way to train a new worker is to have him watch a good worker at the job. A DA **68**

83. Follow-up to see how a worker is doing isn't necessary if he got started in the right way. A DA **8**

84. Even if he thinks it is wrong a supervisor should do whatever his boss tells him to do without questioning it. A DA **7**

85. Criticizing a worker for his mistakes will bring better results than praising him for his good work. A DA **6**

86. The supervisor doing the best job is the one who is always in the shop, loudly pointing out mistakes and spurring the workers on to greater productions. A DA **5**

87. Before deciding on the solution to a problem, a list of possible solutions should be made and compared. A DA **6**

88. A supervisor should keep his boss informed of what's going on. A DA **5**

89. A better understanding of people will result in higher morale and more production. A DA **0**

90. A study of the actions of recognized leaders may greatly increase one's knowledge of leadership. A DA **1**

91. A supervisor should be willing to listen to almost everything the workers want to tell him. A DA **12**

92. A supervisor should have someone trained to take over his job. A DA **4**

93. The worker should look toward the steward and the union for leadership rather than toward the supervisor. A DA **2**

94. The supervisor can do very little to make his workers happy because company policy controls such things as wages, vacations and bonuses. A DA **9**

95. A supervisor should always display a friendly manner towards his workers. A DA **4**

96. The training needs of a department should be determined by the supervisor in charge. A DA **17**

97. A supervisor in a large department should never delegate any of his authority to a subordinate; he should delegate only responsibility. A DA **40**

139

98. A supervisor doesn't have to be a leader if he has all the technical know-how for the job.

A DA

7

99. It pays for the supervisor to spend a lot of time with a new employee to be sure he is well trained on his first job.

A DA

6

100. Courses on Human Relations are of very little value. We should be learning more about the technical aspects of our job.

A DA

6

About Kirkpatrick Partners

Kirkpatrick Partners was founded to help companies create, demonstrate, and measure true business value through their training and major initiatives.

Kirkpatrick Partners is proud to be directly owned and operated by Don, Jim and Wendy Kirkpatrick. When you work with us, you get authentic materials from The One and Only Kirkpatrick^{SM}.

Kirkpatrick Partners offers the following programs and services:

Seminars

- Kirkpatrick Business Partnership Certification Program
- Kirkpatrick Four Level Evaluation Certification and Certificate Programs
- Training On Trial
- And others

Custom Training Events and Keynotes

We are happy to work with you to customize a message or program appropriate for your event or group.

Consulting

Obtain a custom training methodology from the Kirkpatricks

Register on our Website to Receive:

- Access to free articles, white papers, diagrams, and podcasts
- Subscription to our monthly e-newsletter

KIRKPATRICKPARTNERS.COM

KIRKPATRICK PARTNERS
The one and only KIRKPATRICK™

ABOUT DON KIRKPATRICK, PH.D.

Dr. Donald L. Kirkpatrick holds B.A., M.A., and Ph.D. degrees from the University of Wisconsin in Madison.

At the Management Institute of the University of Wisconsin, Don taught managers at all levels the principles and techniques of many subjects including Coaching, Communication, Managing Time, Managing Change, Team Building, and Leadership.

In industry, Don served as Training Director for International Minerals and Chemical Corp. where he developed a Performance Appraisal Program. Later he served as Human Resources Manager of Bendix Products Aerospace Division.

Don is a past national president of the American Society For Training and Development (ASTD) where he received the Gordon Bliss and "Lifetime Achievement in Workplace Learning and Performance" awards. He is a member of Training Magazine's Hall Of Fame. In 2007, he received the "Lifetime Achievement Award" from the Asia HRD Congress.

Don is the author of seven Management Inventories and seven books including the 3rd edition of *Evaluating Training Programs: The Four Levels,* which has become the basis for evaluation all over the world. This book has been translated into Spanish, Polish, Turkish, and Chinese. His other books include: *Implementing the Four Levels, Transferring Learning to Behavior, Developing Employees Through Appraisal and Coaching* 2nd edition (2006); *How To Plan and Conduct Productive Meetings* (2006); and *Managing Change Effectively* (2002).

Don is a regular speaker at national conferences of ASTD, IQPC, Nielsen (Training Magazine), and other professional and company conferences. He is a frequent speaker at ASTD chapters.

For more information about Don and his work, visit kirkpatrickpartners.com and linkedin.com/in/donaldkirkpatrick.

Don can be contacted at don.kirkpatrick@kirkpatrickpartners.com.

Made in the USA
Charleston, SC
26 May 2010